རྒྱལ་སྤྱིའི་བོད་ཀྱི་གསོ་རིག་ཁང་།

SORIG KHANG
INTERNATIONAL
www.sorig.net

Weapon of Light

INTRODUCTION TO
Ati Yoga Meditation

Nida Chenagtsang

SKY
PRESS

Published by:

SKY PRESS

3640 SE Washington Street
Portland, OR 97214
www.skypressbooks.com

Library of Congress Control Number: 2017947454

ISBN
978-0-9977319-6-5

Editor: Christiana Polites
Translation: Ben Joffe (Jigmé Dorje)
Design and Typeset: Pearse Gaffney

First English Edition
Printed on acid-free paper

Special thanks to all whose valuable contributions
made this work possible.

CONTENTS

Mönmo Tashi Chidren

Dedication

I dedicate the *Weapon of Light* to all female practitioners: to my teacher Ani Ngawang Gyaltsen and to all nuns and yoginis in order to empower women to liberate themselves and others through the practice of Ati Yoga. I especially dedicate *Weapon of Light* to the great eighth century female master, Mönmo Tashi Chidren, and her reincarnation Khandro Tshering Chödron whose blessings were the direct inspiration behind this work. May it help beginner practitioners to start their meditation and may it serve as a reminder to experienced practitioners of how to maintain the Ati Yoga state in daily life.

- *Nida Chenagtsang*

PUBLISHER'S PREFACE

In November 2016, SKY Press published its first book, *Mirror of Light: A Commentary on Yuthok's Ati Yoga, Volume One* by Dr. Nida Chenagtsang. This book presents in a very precise and traditional manner the view and meditation of *Dzogchen trekchöd* ('cutting through hardness') practice. Because in *trekchöd* practice the view is of utmost importance, Dr. Nida reinforced the view by supplementing Yuthok Yönten Gönpo's original root text, *The Self-Liberation of Samsara - Nirvana*, with his own explanations and many quotations from Tibet's great Ati Yoga masters of the past. *Mirror of Light* points the reader back again and again to the present fresh and luminous awareness which is one's basic state. As Yuthok taught:

"Perceive the primordial mind-essence which does not arise, cease, or abide, that is free of the stain of limiting conceptions, of mental elaborations, of center and periphery. It is not composed of any essential nature at all – though it appears as diverse and radiant arisings, even as it arises it lacks anything that arises

with either basis or root. Allow this naked and vividly present awareness which is beyond all and every mental reification, beyond speaking or imagining, which is inconceivable and ineffable, to freely unfold. It is completely relaxed and open, it is all outer appearances, all inner awareness without exception, it is utterly unobstructed wisdom, which has no need to reject the bad afflictive emotions usually meant to be rejected. Perceive this natural state that appears imperceptibly as the natural state of primordial is-ness, let the unchanging wisdom of experiential awareness arise deep in one's mind. Loosen up into the fresh and spontaneous presence of the sheer suchness of walking, moving around, lying down, and sitting, of body, speech, mind, and all actions, into totally free, uncontrived, and natural self-radiance. Sustain a state of being that is merely undistracted, naked, and completely relaxed and open. Practicing like this, your own mind will actually be transformed into the mind of Samantabhadra, and its arising as the body of absolute-reality itself will be brought to completion.'

Following the release of *Mirror of Light*, Dr. Nida traveled to the United States and introduced the profound teachings held in this book in six locations across the country – in bookstores, in dharma centers, in healing centers, in social and academic clubs, in big cities and in small towns, in the desert, in the mountains, on the beach…

To match the diversity of the venues was an equally diverse selection of attendees, from the absolute beginner meditator who happened to be browsing the bookstore at the time of the talk, to the highly experienced dharma practitioner. Dr. Nida's talks were colloquial, simple, pithy, and deep, and brought the traditional teachings from *Mirror of Light* out into a modern context in a highly practical and direct way that everyone could understand and benefit from. These talks were the inspiration behind this book and form the introductory material. In order to preserve Dr. Nida's voice and direct and practical teaching style when he gives oral instruction, the transcripts of these talks were edited only very slightly by the publisher.

The core teachings of this book are contained in Dr Nida's beautiful Tibetan poem entitled *The Weapon of Light of the Primordial Wisdom which Vanquishes the Darkness of Samsara* which he composed shortly after this *Mirror of Light* book tour while traveling in Japan. His intention in sharing these verses is to directly guide practitioners, both beginner and experienced on how to access and maintain the Ati Yoga state in daily life – when one's mind is naturally at rest, when one's mind is in motion under the sway of the afflictive emotions, and when one is in the state of pure awareness.

"If you try to get rid of thoughts,
they will just increase.
Instead, look at their essence, at their true face,
without throwing away your meditation
in the process.
At times thoughts vanish and at times they proliferate,
If you meditate continually,
they will gradually be pacified.

Even if you don't let thoughts go, they go anyway.
Even if you don't hold onto them,
they cling to you anyway.
Even if you don't incite them,
they move around and are agitated anyway.
Whatever they do, look directly at their essence
and just leave them as they are."

The final chapter of this text is the mind instruction that Padmasambhava gave to Mönmo Tashi Chidren, the eighth century female master and devotee of Yeshe Tsogyal to whom Dr. Nida has dedicated this work. The juxtaposition and at the same time continuity between traditional *terma* (treasure) teachings and Dr. Nida's modern presentation of Ati Yoga teachings is one of the unique features of *Weapon of Light*. Ati Yoga teachings are timeless.

Garab Dorje taught *Dzogchen* in three steps: introduction, decision, and confidence. In one of his oral teachings on the *Mirror of Light* book tour, Dr. Nida explained that the introduction is the pointing out that our mind is light by a qualified teacher. This pointing out is very simple and direct, but due to our habitual tendency to fall into doubts, it takes time and effort to come to the clear decision that our mind's nature is light – pristine wisdom, bliss, and joy. Light requires force, and the decision is the force that empowers the introduction. *Weapon of Light* is this force which brings us back again and again in a very sharp, cutting, direct, and experiential way to our mind's true empty and luminous nature, until unshakable confidence is naturally born within us. This confidence in our true state is the root of liberation.

Traditionally Ati Yoga teachings are given orally by the teacher and then contemplated again and again by the student. Often the instructions were sung so as to allow the teachings to sink into one's energetic channels. In order to enhance this capacity of contemplation and self-reflection, we created an audio book with chanting of Dr. Nida's Tibetan verses by Drukmo Gyal Dakini, music by Tamding Arts, and an English reading of the text. Drukmo Gyal's beautiful voice and slow and calming melodies lull the mind into a very relaxed state in which the meaning of the text can then permeate one's mind stream and subtle body in a deep and direct way. A digital download of this audio file can be purchased from the SKY Press website. A free download of the English only reading is also available on the website. Especially during challenging times, listening to the audio of these teachings can be incredibly beneficial. As Dr. Nida says, please 'use the weapon!'

I would like to extend my gratitude to our fantastic SKY Press team – to Ben Joffe (Jigmé Dorje) for his excellent translation of Dr. Nida's Tibetan verses and Guru Rinpoche's mind teaching to Mönmo Tashi Chidren, as well as for his help with the final edits of this text; to Pearse Gaffney for his modern graphics that capture so well the spirit of this *Weapon of Light*; and most of all to Dr. Nida for this precious teaching and his continual reminder of the light within.

Christiana Polites
Portland, Oregon, June 2017
SKY Press
www.skypressbooks.com
info@skypressbooks.com

What is Ati Yoga?

One of the most important questions we can ask ourselves in this life is "Who am I?" In Tibetan, Buddhism is often referred to as *nangdön rigpa*, or the "Inner Science," and we can think of the Buddha's teachings as a set of precise methods for investigating the inner worlds of our human potential. Turning inwards to analyze our consciousness, to discover the basic nature of our mind – this is the common thread that runs through all Buddhist practices. In the oldest school of Tibetan Buddhism, Ati Yoga is the name given to the highest teaching for discovering who we are. It is the most direct method for realizing our ultimate nature.

So what does Ati Yoga mean, exactly? The Tibetan translation for the Sanskrit word 'Yoga' is *naljor* (རྣལ་འབྱོར་ *rnal 'byor*). *Nal* (short for *nalma*) means the pure, primordial or original state – the most basic or uncontrived condition of being – and *jor* means to receive, to get, to arrive at, or to connect or unite with. The Tibetan word shows us clearly what yoga is all about. To be a practitioner of yoga – to be a yogi (male) or yogini (female) means you are someone who does special practices to get back to the pure state, it means you are someone who returns from a contaminated state to a more original or pure condition.

We can think of this in terms of outer, more material phenomena like the five elements of traditional Indian, Tibetan, and Greek philosophy. What is the original state of these elements? What is 'original' space, fire, air, earth, water? Today, in the 21st century with all our pollution it might be hard for us to imagine original, pure air or oxygen. It's the same with water – originally the water on our planet was a pure element but today because of human activities, water has become polluted and stagnant. At one time our planet was perfect but now because of our own ignorance and greed we have messed it up and have polluted our air and contaminated our earth and waters. The best solution for this problem would be if we could find some way to filter or purify these elements and return them to their original pure state. Just think – can you imagine what our planet would be like without humans – 200,000 years ago before the influence of human contamination?

In the Yoga tradition we talk about the mind

in a similar way to how we talk about air and water. Today our human mind is contaminated by harmful political, cultural, and religious views and indoctrination; it is polluted by wrong education. We have been brainwashed by the media and a bombardment of information. Our mind is polluted in the same way that the air and the water is polluted. In traditional Buddhist texts, we call this human mind pollution the 'mental afflictions' or 'poisons'. But given how many toxic chemicals we use in our world today, I think the term 'contamination' – 'human mind contamination' – may be even more appropriate than 'affliction'. Our mind is contaminated with feelings and emotions, it is filled with worry, sorrow, depression, sadness and fear. Our mind is full of traumas and dramas and all kinds of dark energy, and our toxic thinking radiates out constantly like dark waves. But what is an unpolluted or uncontaminated mind? According to Ati Yoga, the uncontaminated mind is the mind of light, of pristine wisdom, bliss, and joy. Our mind is naturally full of light, radiant like the sun. This uncontaminated mind of light is called Buddha Mind and it is the original state of our mind that precedes the 'contamination' of ordinary human conceptual thought.

When we talk about mind though, this analogy with the outer elements of our environment doesn't fit completely. Ati Yoga is a Sanskrit term – the Tibetan name for this approach is Dzogchen (ཛྫོགས་ཆེན། rdzogs chen). [I prefer to use the Sanskrit term because it is much easier for non-Tibetans to pronounce. Ati Yoga is all about ease and simplicity, so I think it is only right that its name should be easy for people to say as well!] Even so, the meaning of the Tibetan term Dzogchen is revealing. Dzogchen means the 'Great Perfection' or 'Completion'. This is explained as meaning that the basic or original, pure state of our mind is totally complete – there is nothing that has to be or can be added to or taken away from it. Our Buddha-nature is already perfect as it is. With water or air it is a little bit different: we have to filter it, change it, but with the Ati Yoga approach for mind we are not trying to fix anything.

One way to understand this is through the analogy of sleeping and waking up. Nal, the primordial pure state of mind, is the Buddha mind. The word Buddha means to 'wake up!' We have Buddha mind, we have always had it and it has always been completely perfect and completely pure, but this Buddha mind is sleeping while our contaminated mind is awake. That is our problem – the crazy part is awake while the wise part sleeps. When we are asleep, the waking quality of our mind remains present, it is just dormant. If we become lucid in our dream, for example, it is not that some sort of waking part that we didn't have before is added to our mind. When we wake up, we don't need to go through the whole process of cleaning, filtering, and transforming our mental poisons or the confusion that makes us forget we are in a dream – we simply wake up to our mind's innate lucidity or wakefulness. That is why it is taught that Ati Yoga is the swiftest way to reach the awakened state, the most direct way to achieve Buddhahood and wake up from the slumber of ignorance.

What then is the meaning of Ati? Very simply put, Ati means "extreme." Ati Yoga is thus the 'Extreme Yoga'. Many people translate Ati as 'supreme' or 'ultimate' but I prefer 'extreme.' Some people might find this interpretation a little surprising. It is true after all that many Buddhist philosophies say, 'Don't be extreme, don't be extreme!' But what about today's societies? Our societies are extreme! And what about the extent of our mental pollution? We suffer from extreme mental pollution and contamination. Everything is extreme! If we compare this century to the last one, it is very extreme and if we compare the last century to the one that came before it, it was also extreme. Societies today are speeding up, becoming more and more extreme. These days, if you tell people, "Don't be extreme, go slowly," it doesn't work. If you tell people, "Don't get excited, keep calm, be quiet," it doesn't work because our society is barreling ahead like a giant wave in an ocean. If you're in the middle of a tsunami, you can't tell people to keep quiet and relax. During an earthquake, you can't say, "Don't run away, just stay here!" It doesn't work that way. That's why Padmasambhava, the great 8th Century Indian Buddhist master who founded Tibetan Vajrayana Buddhism, said that Ati Yoga is the only meditation that will save humans. It doesn't matter how much society will change and it doesn't matter how much the times will change, Ati Yoga will always be suitable for discovering our true nature. In fact, Padmasambhaba said that the darker and more confused the times, the greater the degeneration, the greater the power that Ati Yoga will have to liberate people's minds.

Padmasambhava was an extreme master himself. He taught nine different levels or 'vehicles' of teaching as part of his Nyingma school, the earliest school of Tibetan Buddhism. The first three vehicles are very slow and the next three are also not so fast. The last three vehicles are called the three 'inner yogas.' These, according to the Ati Yoga master Longchenpa, are the antidotes for the three mental poisons – the first is Maha Yoga, the antidote for anger, the second is Anu Yoga, the antidote for desire, and the last one is Ati Yoga, the antidote for ignorance or confusion. As the fastest and most direct path, Ati Yoga is also the most suitable for our modern, speedy times. It is the ninth vehicle, the highest practice, but as Padmasambhava explained, it is not necessarily a requirement that we go step by step through the practices in a linear manner. If you understand Ati Yoga then all other practices of all other vehicles are contained within it. So, if you want to focus on just one practice, you should focus on Ati Yoga. If you do other practices as well, then Ati Yoga is like a great enhancer, it does not contradict any other practice, but enhances and reframes all of them. For example, if you do a deity practice, such as Tara practice, you shouldn't stop doing that practice, but if you do Ati Yoga meditation, you will have a deeper understanding of Tara. You will understand that all Buddhas exist within Tara and that all Buddhas exist within your own subtle body, energy, and mind – all in one and one in all. When you truly realize your Buddha nature you realize it encompasses everything.

Another reason Ati Yoga is 'extreme yoga' is because it is extremely fast, extremely simple, and extremely effective. There is a quote by Leonardo DaVinci, the great 15th century scientist and inventor that captures this well. DaVinci is purported to have said that "simplicity is the ultimate sophistication." Normally when we think of extreme simplicity, we think of something not so profound or deep, not so vast, not so sophisticated ('simple' in English can even mean stupid!). And yet, even though Ati Yoga is very simple and very direct, as a meditation or spiritual practice it is extremely effective and sophisticated.

This calls to mind another quote from Albert Einstein. He said, 'everything must be simple, as simple as possible – but not simpler.' Einstein was talking about physics but this statement applies perfectly to spiritual traditions as well. Today learning yoga can be so complicated – there are so many rules and postures. Some yogas help your back and some other yogas break your back. There are so many complicated meditations, mantras, and visualizations. According to Ati yoga, however, spirituality must be simple – as simple as possible, but not simpler. It's very important to recognize the simplicity but at the same time incredible sophistication and value of these teachings, as well as the extent of one's personal karma to receive instruction in them. If we don't, it would be like we were a millionaire who dies having only accumulated riches but never having enjoyed them. In ancient times, people recognized the incredible value and rarity of these teachings, so they practiced them with diligence, knowing that their lives too were precious and impermanent. We should have this same attitude today and not fall victim to the modern consumerism mentality in which we want to acquire more and more things, receive many empowerments, practices, and mantras, but don't recognize the profundity of the instruction we have received and truly put it into practice.

The Ati Yoga teachings described in this book are those of Yuthok Yönten Gönpo, Tibet's most famous physician. Yuthok's students, who were mostly doctors as well, were extremely busy. Especially in ancient times, the doctor's work in Tibet was true Bodhisattva activity, pure altruism. Doctors would collect herbs and other ingredients and prepare herbal medicines, they would travel several hours by yak to visit the sick in faraway places, they would receive patients at their homes day and night. There was no personal time for oneself, all of one's energy was dedicated towards helping others. Because Yuthok understood how busy his students were, he offered them an extremely clear and extremely condensed version of Ati Yoga as his last teaching. He taught various guru yogas and the traditional six yogas as well, of course, and he taught these practices in a very concise and essential way too, but Ati Yoga was his final teaching, his final gift to us.

Introduction, Decision, and Confidence

In the famous Ati Yoga text, *The Three Statements that Strike the Vital Point*, Garab Dorje taught three axioms: Pointing Out ('direct introduction to one's nature), Decision ('directly and definitively deciding upon this state', and Confidence ('gaining confidence in the immediacy of liberation.' The pointing out is the introduction to the true nature of your mind. What is the nature of the mind? It is infinite light and infinite bliss. The essence of human mind is light. All that we see, all that we hear, all that we feel, smell, and taste – all of these feelings and sensations are simply light experience. Inside the infinite clear light of our mind, there are some bubbles and waves which are our thoughts and emotions. The light is creating a kind of tsunami or a typhoon, but if you know that it is just light, there's no disturbance, no problem. It is only when you don't recognize the thoughts and emotions as light that these waves can disturb you. When you contemplate this light again and again, it increases and then all the dark waves of our negative thoughts and emotions dissolve into light and become light. Ati Yoga is that easy. The clear light that is the nature of your own mind is your own inner guru. You are born with this guru, you live with this guru all the time, and you die with this guru. This guru is more important than any external guru. The external guru is there to point you to the experience of your own inner guru, this clear and vast luminosity.

According to the Ati Yoga tradition, strong emotions are good because when you experience them your mind is not scattered everywhere, you naturally become very focused. Ati Yoga says that anger is a clear light, an energy, a vibration. Once you really grab it and look inside of it, you see that it is just a light, an infinite light. Soon you will begin to actually like anger and all of the disturbing emotions, because you will see them as an opportunity. But when you meditate on them, these emotions do not stay, they simply dissolve into the light and are self-liberated.

Yuthok said that when you are sad, your meditation works better. This took time for me to understand. Normally when you are sad and experience loneliness or grief, it is the basis for depression. But Yuthok says, when you are sad, that is the best moment to practice Ati Yoga. You don't need to visualize the Buddha, you don't need to recite mantras, you don't need to do rituals or read texts, you just look directly into the sadness. What is this sadness? It is light. If you are very present and if you can meditate on that sadness, you can go into a very deep and profound state. If you penetrate the sadness, you will see that it is actually an immense luminous space – blissful, joyful, and silent. This is why Yuthok said that sadness is the best emotion for Ati Yoga. Just don't be obsessed with sadness. Don't get attached to it but don't refuse it either – whether sadness is there or not, you can always be in this state of vast luminous space. Whether anger, fear, jealousy, desire, or pride arise or not, your mind is a vast luminous space. This is the pointing out, or introduction to your mind's true nature.

We must be introduced to the nature of our mind as luminosity by a qualified teacher, but making the firm decision and gaining the confidence in that decision depends on us. Ati Yoga confronts us with the key question, with one simple decision: do we want to stay in the darkness or would we rather be in the light? Do we choose bliss or do we choose suffering? Because we are so habituated to staying in the darkness, it requires effort and practice to make a firm decision and gain conviction in our light – we must train with our body, our speech (energy), and our mind. The Tibetan word *jang* (སྦྱང་ *sbyang*) means both to train and to purify, so the process of training purifies our body and energy of illnesses and blockages and cleans our mind of wrong views, obscurations, and misperceptions so that we can see our true nature clearly and continuously.

In the Ati Yoga tradition, can we train our bodies using one simple physical posture, our energy with breathing exercises, and our mind with the analytical meditation of investigating the arising, abiding, and cessation of thoughts and emotions. This training, which must be repeated again and again until it becomes very familiar, reinforces the introduction so that any doubts and confusion may be eliminated and confidence in the decision becomes firm. Then the liberation comes by itself.

The Vajra Posture:
for the Body Training preliminary practice

1: BODY

Vajra Posture

According to the Ati Yoga tradition, we have the potential for infinite energy because our mind is full of infinite light. Our energy is generated from the mind which is exactly like the sun, radiant and powerful. Darkness and light cannot coexist; if you try to bring darkness close to the sun it will be instantly transformed into light. The nature of our mind is exactly like the sun, it has the power to transform all darkness into light, to dissolve all negative thoughts and emotions.

Our body is called the Vajra Body and it has the same power and light as our mind. This is why humans have the potential to attain rainbow body, the complete dissolution of the material body into light as in the case of Padmasambhava and both Yuthok the Elder and Yuthok the Younger. Rainbow body or *Jalu* in Tibetan (འཇའ་ལུས་ *'ja lus*) is the sign of complete spiritual realization and mastery of the physical elements. It is the total transformation of body, energy, and mind, which is the direct result of the practice of Ati Yoga.

Vajra (Tibetan: *Dorje*, རྡོ་རྗེ་ *rdo rje*) means 'diamond' or 'indestructible' – the nature of our body is indestructible, like a diamond, with a force like nuclear power. It has the power to dissolve all darkness. We only experience our body as weak and limited because we have not trained it and recognized it's infinite potential. Our body contains 72,000 energy channels which in our ordinary state are blocked and knotted. When we train the body through physical yoga practices we untie these knots and release the blockages so that energy can flow freely. When the energy flows freely through open channels, the mind naturally relaxes.

In order to train and purify our physical body in the Ati Yoga tradition, there is no need for many complicated body postures and exercises. Only one simple yogic posture is required, called the Vajra Posture, in which you position your body in the form of a vajra by joining your palms together above the crown of your head, and balance with your knees deeply bent and heels lifted and pressing together. While holding the posture, imagine your body to be the ritual instrument, a five pronged radiantly luminous blue vajra.

At the beginning it is very challenging, when you try to hold the posture for some time your body becomes quickly exhausted, you tremble

and you sweat. But this exhaustion has a purpose – when your body becomes exhausted and worn out, the mind releases its tight grip and it naturally relaxes and enters the nondual state. Another meaning of the word Vajra is nondual. While you are training in this posture, the heat and discomfort that is generated from holding the position burns up physical illnesses, wrongdoings, obscurations, and provocations. As the great fifth Dalai Lama explained:

> "It purifies obscurations and pacifies obstacles
> of the body and eliminates attachments...
> it prevents the body from falling into samsara
> and liberates one's body into an emanation body.
> Ultimately it causes the body to pass beyond
> suffering into the Vajra-expanse."
>
> - The Fifth Dalai Lama, Mirror of Light, p.107

Once you get used to this posture, you can hold it for twenty or thirty minutes without feeling any pain or fatigue. This is a sign that you have mastered the posture and purified your physical body. This posture makes the body immortal, like a diamond, completely indestructible. Then you experience the nuclear power of your own physical body, you experience both your body and mind to be the radiant and pure force of the sun.

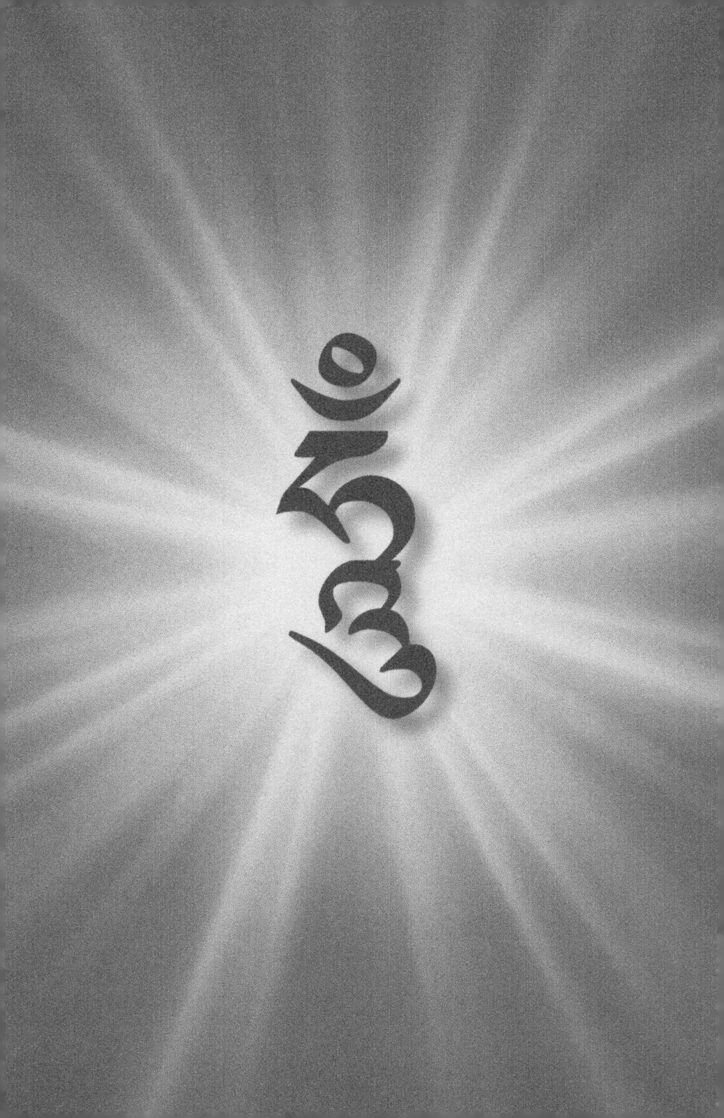
ཧཱུྃ

2: ENERGY/ SPEECH

Vajra Chanting

In Ati Yoga we train our speech with the mantra OM AH HUNG, known as the 'king of mantras'. The OM, AH, and HUNG syllables represent the enlightened qualities of the body, speech, and mind of all the Buddhas. When we talk about 'speech' in Buddhism, we aren't just talking about words or uttered statements – speech implies something broader and more subtle than this, namely 'energy', and energy is always connected with our breathing. The ancient Greek word for breath or air is *pneuma*. There is a common misconception that there is no concept of 'energy' in Western traditions, but the Ancient Greeks used the term *pneuma* to refer both to breath and to 'spirit.' They understood the connection between breath and energy. In China, they speak of *qi*, in India it is called *prana*, in Tibetan we call it *loong* (རླུང་ *rlung*), or wind energy. It would seem that all cultures have or have had a concept of energy that is very closely related to the breath. We have both 'karmic' or ordinary winds and 'wisdom' or enlightened winds in our bodies – the karmic winds run through the 72,000 channels while the wisdom winds are contained in our central channel. When the body and energy are trained and the mind is awakened through Ati Yoga meditation, the karmic winds, which cause discursive thinking, enter into the central channel and are transformed into wisdom wind, giving rise to the nondual experience. Then all of our energy becomes wisdom wind energy.

In order to purify our speech and energy directly, we can practice mantras or we can work with our breath. In Ati Yoga, it is not necessary to recite long or complicated mantras, we use the most basic mantra, the one we are born with that naturally occurs through the simple act of breathing. As we inhale, our breath makes the subtle sound of OM; as we pause our breath at the top of the inhale, there is a naturally occurring AH sound; and as we exhale, our breath hums the sound of HUNG. To enhance the power of this ever-present mantra, we train in it by practicing Vajra Chanting, the 'indestructible chanting'.

To begin, sit with your spine straight: inhale

slowly to the count of five; then gently hold the breath for the count of three; exhale to the count of four. As you breathe like this, tune into the subtle sound of this mantra riding your breath. Strongly hear and sense the OM as you inhale, the AH as you hold your breath and the HUNG as you exhale. If you like, visualize that as you breathe in, white light enters slowly into your body through your nostrils; as you retain the breath, the white light turns to red and expands, filling the whole body with radiant red light; as you breathe out the red light turns to blue and leaves your body through the nostrils.

As you get familiar with this Vajra Chanting, slowly increase the length of the breath retention and the exhale so that all parts of the breath are of equal length: inhale to the count of five, hold for five, exhale for five. As you continue to train in this Vajra Chanting, slowly increase the duration of the retention: for example, inhale five, hold ten, exhale five. When you can effortlessly extend the breath retention and hold for longer and longer periods of time, it is a sign that your energy body and channels are being purified through the training, and your karmic winds are being transformed into wisdom winds.

As a post-meditation exercise in daily life, start observing your speech and your dialogue with others. Notice how conditioned our language is by the word 'I.' According to Buddhist teachings, it is this 'I' and our obsessive fixation on it that is the root of samsara, the source of all our suffering. Train your speech by beginning to cut back on the use of this word 'I' in your daily interactions with others, shifting the emphasis of your speech away from I, me, and mine. Train your speech in this way until your mind also begins to think less about this 'I' and the narrow focus of your attention expands so that your perception of your life and circumstances becomes something expansive and beautiful.

Investigating the Mind

"If you do not inquire into your own mind, whatever virtuous spiritual practices you have undertaken will not hit the vital point. This thing called mind is full of moving activity. If you chase after it you cannot grasp it, it vanishes and dissolves. If you try to put it somewhere it will not rest, but fidgets to and fro. This thing, this so-called mind of yours, is without exact location, is utterly empty and pervasive, yet it is the experiencer of a myriad of joys and sufferings. Look (and see): from whence does this mind first arise?... From whence is it first born? Where does it currently abide? What shape does it have? When in the end thoughts have vanished from the basic ground of their own inherent condition, ask yourself – to where have they disappeared? To where have they gone? Minutely analyze – when thoughts have expired, how is it that they have passed away? Analyze the birthing and the expiring, the coming and going of thoughts. Investigate until you establish for yourself definitively mind's unidentifiable emptiness and inexpressible, totally liberated purity."

- From Flight of the Garuda by Shabkar Tsokdruk Rangdrol (as quoted by Dr. Nida Chenagtsang in Mirror of Light, p.115)

According to the Ati Yoga tradition, we divide our mental analytical meditation into three parts: Jung (ཇུང་ byung) which means the 'source' refers to where thoughts and the mind come from, to their origin; né (གནས་ gnas) means where or how thoughts and the mind stay or abide, and dro (འགྲོ་ 'gro) is concerned with where thoughts, feelings and impressions go or have gone. If you are experiencing an emotion such as sadness, you have to ask – where did that sadness come from? Where is it now? Where is the anxiety that is occurring now? When it is gone and it remains only as a memory, where has it gone to? You have to search for these seemingly concrete, self-evident things to see where they came from and where they went. Did you find its origin in your head or heart? Where did it abide? Was it one clear thing in one single location, could you pin-point it exactly?

At the beginning you should investigate gently, because if you go very deeply it can strongly trigger the emotion, and you might experience the anxiety or the sadness or fear that you are searching for too intensely. So you start softly, but little by little you go deeper and investigate more thoroughly. You search inside your body, inside your brain, inside your head chakra. Where is the emotion or feeling? You must analyze and keep looking, again and again. In Ati Yoga, it is taught that if you investigate carefully enough you will discover through direct experience that there is no ultimate origin, no resting place, nor any place where thoughts and feelings disappear to. But you must experience this for yourself over and over again. Sometimes you search and you say superficially, 'I can't find anything' but when the anxiety comes back, you feel and experience it again because the root is still there. This means you have not searched deeply enough, you must keep repeating the meditation, analyzing and investigating until true insight dawns.

You can search in a very medical and methodical way: if you think the anxiety dwells in your heart, then you should dissect your heart, look in your muscles, vessels, blood, then search on a cellular level, even break down the cells, look at your proteins, your salt, your vitamins and minerals, everything. Do this again and again, then one day when you ask, 'where is the anxiety'? you will see truly that it has no origin, there is no place in which that anxiety dwells, and no place where it has disappeared to. At that point it means you are truly free from anxiety. You see that the anxiety was just your mind's energy manifesting – all the disturbing emotions you experience are just energetic blockages which are manifesting. When you meditate, look inside and search thoroughly for these feelings, thoughts and emotions which arise, and when you fail to find them anywhere, it means they are liberated. Then you are free.

The Ati Yoga tradition says: 'not finding anything is the greatest found discovery'. If you find some 'thing', it means you are still stuck. If you think you can locate something in your body and you feel there is a tension or a dark spot, then this is called a blockage. But when you go deeper and deeper inside that blockage, you come to see that there is actually nothing there, and there never was anything there. Where is your fear? You think the fear is in your head or heart, you feel some kind of pain there, so you meditate and meditate until one day you can't find any fear to hold onto. Ati Yoga says that all these thoughts and emotions are just an illusion. We are trapped in a big illusion; that is the problem and the more we believe in the illusion, the more we believe in thoughts and emotions, feelings and sensations, the more they become solid, concrete. In a dream, if you see a concrete house, you really believe it is made of concrete. But if you become lucid in the dream, you say, "wait this is not concrete – there's no cement, there's no house, there's not even any independent dream 'self' – this is just a dream, the expression or unfolding display of mind which is only light, one big luminous movie!" When you are not lucid, you see and experience solid concrete, when you are lucid, you know it is only light.

All of our emotions and feelings are exactly the same. When you are stuck with depression, the feeling is so heavy and hard, just like concrete. The mind is so powerful, depression is so powerful, it makes everything contract and contract and creates blockage, so of course you feel tension and pain in the chest or in the head. This is the mind's capacity to create psychosomatic problems. Your psyche's power has so much influence over you. But what Ati Yoga teachings are saying is – go into the *soma*, go into your body, find what is blocking you, look for it, investigate it. If you look thoroughly, you are unable to find anything anywhere.

Here is a traditional example: imagine that you are outside of a dark room and you are looking inside, but you cannot see anything because it is dark. You hear all kinds of sounds coming from this room and some people are telling you there is a thief inside, others say there are wild animals making noises, some say it is a demon. You cannot see for yourself, so you can only imagine these robbers, demons, or wild animals. Your mind is so busy creating stories, creating every kind of Hollywood and Bollywood movie, you are receiving a bombardment of conflicting and frightening information from other people telling you what is inside. Ati Yoga says, 'open the door, turn on the light, and look inside!' If you open the door, turn on the light and you look inside, you see that actually there is nothing there, nothing ever was there. So what were all those noises you heard? When you look, you notice that the window is open, and it was just the sound of the wind you were hearing. Your hundreds of thousands of thoughts, fears, imaginations, everything vanishes instantly because you have entered, turned on the light and seen for yourself that the room is empty. There are no demons, no thieves nor wild animals, only the sound of the wind. At this point, your mind is not trapped anymore, it no longer gets lost in all these feelings, emotions, fears, and imaginations. Everything was your projection. You are clear. Ati Yoga has made you clear and fearless.

There is another story that illustrates this point. Once there was a famous Tibetan master who was well known as a great meditator. He was a monk and he meditated all the time in his room, so he thought he was able to process all of his emotions. One day his teacher sent him to meditate in a cave instead. The monk didn't realize until he went to that cave that he had a very deep fear of being there. The first night when it started to get dark, this fear arose and his mind became very busy, imagining all kinds of wild animals coming in to attack him. When it became completely dark, he started to worry about the dampness and cold. He tried to meditate, but his mind was so restless and distracted, he started to became a little crazy. He heard a strange voice, someone calling him, saying 'hello' and his terror overtook him. He was sure he was not hallucinating, was sure this was the real live demon. His heart was pounding as he waited for this demon to come inside his cave. There was absolutely nothing he could do about it, no way to escape into the cold dark night – he was trapped. At that point he accepted fully that someone would really come in and attack him and that the only solution was to meditate, to *really* meditate. He looked inside, tried to grab hold of that powerful fear, and the terror forced him into a state of perfect concentration until he felt something release inside of him and totally relax. This fear never came back, he penetrated it fully and released it and could stay night after night in this cave. Later he realized that this voice was just an owl, and that the fear was transforming the voice of this night bird into a demon. Without this strong fear, he would not have had access to this experience of deep meditation. That's why these strong emotions are considered blessings and opportunities. Without them, sometimes we think we are meditating well, but our practice is merely superficial. If we are able to search and search and penetrate intense emotions like fear and anger, then we are brought directly into their vast and luminous nature which is none other than the luminous space of our own mind.

Rigpa: Pure Awareness

Investigate all your thoughts and emotions, search for them and see for yourself that there is nothing to grasp on to and nothing to reject. Then perceive directly the fresh awareness:

"(Perceive) the primordial mind-essence, which does not arise, cease, or abide, that is free of the stain of limiting conceptions, of mental elaborations of center and periphery. It is not composed of any essential nature at all – though it appears as diverse and radiant arisings, even as it arises it lacks anything that arises with either basis or root. Allow this naked and vividly present awareness which is beyond all and every mental reification, beyond speaking or imagining, which is inconceivable and ineffable, to freely unfold. It is completely relaxed and open, it is all outer appearances, all inner awareness without exception, it is utterly unobstructed wisdom, which has no need to reject the bad and afflictive emotions usually meant to be rejected. Perceive this natural state (that appears) imperceptibly as the natural state of primordial is-ness, let the unchanging wisdom of experiential awareness arise deep in one's mind. Loosen up into the fresh

and spontaneous presence of the sheer suchness of walking, moving around, lying down, and sitting, of body, speech, mind and all actions, into totally free, uncontrived, and natural self-radiance. Sustain a state of being that is merely undistracted, naked, and completely relaxed and open. Practicing like this, your own mind will be actually transformed into the mind of Samantabhadra, and its arising as the body of absolute-reality itself will be brought to completion."

- Yuthok Yönten Gönpo, Mirror of Light, p.161

As a practical exercise, divide time into three parts: past, future and present. Look to your past and examine all the dramas and traumas that you hold as memories. Look into the future and observe all your future worries, plans, hopes and fears. Then observe the present moment and see how the mind is full of distractions, never resting, always running to and fro. Besides the past, present, and future, there is a fourth state – this is the pure fresh and clear awareness, the here and now which is free from subject and object and in which everything is perfect. This is called *rigpa* (རིག་པ་ *rig pa*), the pure awareness. In Ati Yoga practice, we must strip the mind of past dramas and traumas, of present distractions, and of future concerns, and rest in the fourth state, in *rigpa*, in our natural intelligence or spontaneous, pure awareness. Once you recognize this fourth state, then you should look directly at the mind that is observing. You should search for the mind itself until you see that in fact there is no observer – when you realize this, then the boundary between subject and object completely dissolves. The space inside of you – which is far from being just an 'empty' space, but is rather an infinite luminous expanse of great bliss – is unified with the space that encompasses the universe. There is no longer any duality between the appearances outside and the *rigpa* inside.

The Three Restings:
Body, Eyes, Mind

To encourage and enhance the experience
of rigpa, go into the nature, preferably on a
mountain top with a vast and open clear blue
sky and meditate:

Let your body rest, sitting as it is,
relaxed, like a mountain
Let your eyes rest without moving,
as they are, like the ocean
Let your mind rest, as it is,
in its natural awareness

Through these three restings, and without
any inclination for dualistic phenomena,
for what appears or arises in
Samsara or Nirvana – for self and other,
here and there,
good or bad, hopes or doubts, rejecting or accepting,
near or far, sending out or retaining – take as your
practice the all perfected display of wisdom,
the Great Self-Liberation of Samsara - Nirvana."

- Yuthok Yönten Gönpo, Mirror of Light, p.183

Your body is stable and still like a mountain; your eyes are clear and vivid like a limpid sea; your thoughts flow freely like a river, all the dramas and traumas of the past flow by like rushing water, do not try to grasp hold of them, let them go. Your ultimate self awareness is unchangeable, radiant, clear, and vivid, like the cloudless sky.

Conclusion: Expansion

Do you know how many neurons we have in our brains? Neuroscientists tell us we have trillions of neurons, but we don't believe or experience this. We think because our memory is so poor and because it is difficult to study, maybe we have only ten neurons, or even just one stupid neuron banging around in our heads that makes up 'me'. But if you open your mind and you trust the neuroscientists, then you know that you have trillions of neurons, and that each one of them is so powerful. If you could take your brain from out of your skull and throw it outside, it could become a whole galaxy, and one galaxy contains trillions of stars. That's why in the Ati Yoga teachings, it says that openness and expansion is very important. Just open, open, and open, expand and expand, and then all of these trillions of stars, they are your stars, because you are the galaxy. Everything that exists, everything that occurs, all apparent phenomena are reflections in the luminous mirror of your mind. Don't get stuck with just one planet, saying this is *my* planet, this is *my* star – you have trillions! Why get stuck with one? They are all yours, just open your eyes and know that all that you see and experience is your nature, that everything belongs to you.

When it comes to Dharma practice, we should not get stuck on one Buddha because there are billions of Buddhas, countless Buddhas, and they are all within you. When you meditate on one Buddha, you are meditating on billions of Buddhas. Open and open, expand and expand, do not contract and limit your view. We have put our mind into a little box – our little mind here and everyone else's out there. Our imagined self, our heart is encased in a tiny 'capsule' but when we open the capsule the space inside it is unified with the space of the whole universe. The Yuthok Nyingthig doesn't emphasize elaborate meditation deity practice but focuses instead on Guru Yoga. Yuthok warns us not to chase after tantric deities or dakinis. He knew that when we put our mind and our own sense of self into a capsule, our natural inclination, our temptation is to run after yet more capsules: this deity from this lineage and not that one, this dakini, this practice. Once we get fixated on our preferred capsules, once we draw strong lines around things, the process will never end.

All the divisions people make between gurus and religious practices, all the sectarianism we see today is a kind of 'spiritual paranoia'.Yuthok shows us that the point of true Guru Yoga is to open our capsules. Our conventional mind invents capsules separating us from the Guru, from the Buddha.

But Yuthok reminds us that there is no difference whatsoever between the nature of these three – the point of Guru Yoga is to directly experience that your mind, the mind of your Guru, and the mind of the Buddha are all one. Your mind's essence is the same as the Guru's. If you break open your tight capsule, dissolve your drop into the ocean of Buddha mind, the 'you' that you think you know dissolves into the pure open space that contains everything – all deities, all dakinis, all mantras and all practices, everything is there. This is your true human potential. You have everything within you and you can never lose anything. If you meditate in this way, you experience everything. You have energy, you have light, you have stars, you have colors, mantras, Buddhas, whatever you need is present and available. At the moment of death you know that you don't lose anything, because your mind is completely opened. The mind transcends even death. Once you have the Ati Yoga experience, you become fearless because you know that the nature of your mind transcends both time and space.

When you expand your view and your experience, it is no longer about 'I' and 'mine', about 'my' decision, 'my' confidence, 'my' meditation, the process of discovering 'myself', which can all seem so selfish and narrow. With this expansion, you see all the inter-connections between beings and your heart expands and compassion grows. You naturally want others to be free of suffering and to feel this opening too. Today some *Dzogchen* practitioners say that love and compassion – which they label as the more ordinary concerns of 'lower' forms of Mahayana Buddhist teachings – are not important, that they only need to find *rigpa* and what they think of as 'conventional ethics' don't matter. But the depth of this Ati Yoga experience naturally brings love and compassion, it makes you humble and kind, it makes you soft but not weak – soft but very strong, without arrogance.

This humility and kindness is a natural outcome of the Ati Yoga view: when you know everything is encompassed by your mind, then if you don't like something, if you find something unpleasant, there's no point in rejecting it, since it is part of you and your own experience. Likewise, if you like something, what's the point of craving it, when you have it already? The difference between an ordinary human's mind and the mind of a Buddha is that the human mind is full of divisions, is full of constructed boxes. Buddha Mind by contrast is all-pervading and all-inclusive. Through Ati Yoga we learn to open and to expand, and to drop false divisions that separate us from the luminous blissful quality of our own nature and our innate compassion.

The Weapon of Light
of the Primordial Wisdom
which Vanquishes the
Darkness of Samsara

Introduction to Ati Yoga Meditation

སེམས་ཀྱི་གནས་འགྱུ་རིག་གསུམ་གྱི་རྡོ་རྗེ་གནད་བསྲུས་
འཁོར་བའི་མུན་པ་འཇོམས་བྱེད་ཡེ་ཤེས་འོད་ཀྱི་མཚོན་ཆ།

*The Weapon of Light of the Primordial Wisdom
which Vanquishes the Darkness of Samsara:*

*Key Points for Recognizing the (Nature of) Mind in
its Resting, Moving, and Pure-Awareness States.*

བཙོམ་ལྡན་འདས་སངས་རྒྱས་སྨན་གྱི་བླ་མ་སྨན་རྒྱལ་གཡུ་ཐོག་ཡོན་
ཏན་མགོན་པོ་མཆོག་ལ་ཕྱག་འཚལ་ལོ། མཆོད་དོ། སྐྱབས་སུ་མཆིའོ།

I prostrate, give offerings, and go for
Refuge to the Victorious and Transcendent
Medicine Buddha, the King of Doctors,
sublime Yuthok Yönten Gönpo!

ཕྱིར་བསྒོམ་གྱི་གནས་ལུགས་ལ། མདོ་ལུགས་ལ། སེམས་རྟེ་གཅིག་
ཏུ་གནས་པའི་ཞི་གནས་དང་། སེམས་ཀྱི་རྡོ་བོ་གསལ་སྟོང་དབྱེར་མེད་
དུ་མཐོང་བའི་ལྷག་མཐོང་དང་། ལྟ་བ་མཐར་ཕྱུག་རྟེན་དང་འབྲེལ་
འབྱུང་གི་ཞི་ལྷག་ཟུང་འཇུག་བཅས་གསུམ་དང་། སྔགས་ལུགས་
ལ། ཐ་ཐལ་སྡུང་ཞེན་སྐྱོང་བའི་བསྐྱེད་རིམ་དང་རྩ་ཐིག་རླུང་གསུམ་ལ་
མངའ་དབང་བསྒྱུར་བའི་རྫོགས་རིམ་དང་། ལྷུན་སྐྱེས་བདེ་སྟོང་གནས་
ལུགས་རྟོགས་པའི་ བསྐྱེད་རྫོགས་ཟུང་འཇུག་དང་། སྤྲོས་མེད་རྟོགས་
རིམ་མཐར་ཕྱུག་སེམས་ཀྱི་གནས་ལུགས་སྟེ། ལྷུན་སྐྱེས་འོད་གསལ་

གཞུག་སེམས་སྟོན་པའི་ བསྐྱེད་རྫོགས་ཟུང་འཇུག་དང་། སྟོས་མེད་
རྫོགས་རིམ་མཐར་ཕྱུག་སེམས་ ཀྱི་གནས་ལུགས་སྟེ། ལྟུན་སྐྱེས་འོད་
གསལ་གཞུག་སེམས་སྟོན་པའི་ཕྱག་རྒྱ་ཆེན་པོ་དང་། ཡང་ན་སྤྲ་འགྱུར་
ལུགས་ཀྱི་དུག་གསུམ་གྱི་གཉེན་པོ་སྟེ། ཁོང་ཁྲོའི་གཉེན་པོ་རྣལ་འབྱོར་
ཆེན་པོའམ་མ་ད་ཡོ་ག འདོད་ཆགས་གཉེན་པོ་ཕྱུག་བྱུང་རྣལ་འབྱོར་
རས་ཨ་ནུ་ཡོ་ག་དང་གཏི་མུག་གཉེན་པོ་ཤིན་ཏུ་རྣལ་འབྱོར་རས་ཨ་ཏི་
ཡོ་ག་བཅས་ལས།

In general, in the sutric system the ultimate or
basic state dealt with in meditation is threefold:
shinay (Shamata) or 'peaceful abiding' where
the mind abides single-pointedly; *lhagtong* or
'seeing beyond or through' (Vipashyana), where
the mind's essence is perceived as indivisible
clarity-emptiness; and the unification of *shinay*
and *lhagtong* which is the ultimate view of
dependent origination. In the tantric system,
there is *kyerim* or the Creation Stage which
purifies attachments to ordinary appearances;
dzogrim or the Completion Stage which grants
mastery over the channels, drops, and winds; and
the unification of the Creation and Completion
stages where one realizes the underlying and
abiding reality of co-emergent bliss-emptiness.
Then we have the ultimate basic state of the mind
in the unelaborated Creation Stage which is the
Chagya Chenpo or the 'Great Seal' Mahamudra

that reveals the co-emergent light-and-clarity of the innate, natural mind. In addition, in the Old Translation or Nyingma system there are the 'remedies' for each of the three poisons: Maha Yoga or 'The Great Yoga', which is the remedy for anger; Anu Yoga or 'The Pre-eminent Yoga' which is the remedy for desire; and Ati Yoga or the 'Utmost Yoga', which is the remedy for ignorance.

འདིར་སྟོན་འགྲོ་དང་བླ་མའི་རྣལ་འབྱོར་གྱི་ཉམས་ལེན་ལ་གཞོལ་བཞིན་པའི་ཡོ་གི་དང་ཡོ་གི་ནི་རྣམས་ལ་ཕན་པའི་ཆེད་དུ། རྒྱུ་བོ་ཆེ་ཆུང་དང་རིང་ཐུང་འདྲ་མིན་ཐམས་ཅད་གཅིག་ཏུ་འབབ་པའམ་འདུས་པའི་རྒྱ་མཚོ་ཆེན་པོ་ལྟ་བུ། ཀུན་འདུས་མཆར་གྲུབ་གི་བསྒོམ་དོན་ཨ་ཏི་ཡོ་གའི་དོ་སྟོད་དང་ཉམས་ལེན་གྱི་སྙིང་དོན་འགོད་པར་བྱ་སྟེ། སེམས་ཀྱི་གནས་ལུགས་གནས་པ་དང་། འགྱུ་བའམ་འཕྲོ་བ་དང་རང་སོར་རང་དོ་སྟོང་པའམ་རིག་པ་བཅས་ཆ་གསུམ་གྱི་སྒོ་ནས་བསྒོམ་པའི་གནད་བཞད་པར་བྱའོ།

In order to benefit yogis and yoginis who are applying themselves diligently in the preliminary practices and Guru Yoga, like rivers of various sizes and lengths that all flow down or condense together into one great ocean, I have written down here the quintessential meaning of the practices and pointing out processes of Ati Yoga, the ultimate embodiment of the meaning of meditation. In what follows, I explain key points for meditating on the basic state of mind in its three aspects: when it is resting, when it is moving or projecting thoughts, and when it is in a state of rigpa or pure and natural awareness, when it is sustained in its own essence and left naturally just as it is.

Part I

Meditating on the Mind at Rest

དང་པོ། སེམས་གནས་པའི་བསྒོམ།

ལུས་ནི་རྣམ་སྣང་ཆོས་བདུན་ནམ།།
གང་བདེ་སྒལ་ཚིགས་དྲང་པོར་བྱ།།
མིག་ཀྱང་བཙུམ་ཕྱེ་གང་རུང་ལ།།
རླུང་ཡང་ཁ་སྣ་གང་བདེ་བྱ།།

lü ni nam nang chö dün nam
gang dé gel tsik drang por ja
mik kyang tsum ché gang rung la
lung yang kha na gang dé ja

Sit with your body either in
Vairocana's seven-point pose
or straighten your spine as is comfortable.
With your eyes either closed or open,
breathe through your mouth
or your nose as you prefer.

འདས་པ་མ་དྲན་མ་འོངས་མ་བསམ་ལ།།
ད་ལྟ་མི་དཔྱད་མ་གཡེང་ལྷོད་ལ་སྡོད།།
ལུས་ལ་སེམས་གནས་སེམས་ལ་ལྷོད་གནས་པས།།
རང་ཞི་རང་བབ་རང་ལྷོད་གནས་ལུགས་སྐྱོང་།།

dé pa ma dren ma ong ma sam la
da ta mi ché ma yeng lhö la dö
lü la sem né sem la lhö né pé
rang zhi rang bap rang lhö né luk kyong

Without thinking about the past,
fantasizing about the future, or analyzing
the present, sit relaxed, without distraction.
Let your mind remain with the body,
and stay with your mind, loose and relaxed.
Just nurture the innately peaceful, naturally
occurring, intrinsically relaxed state of mind
as-it-is.

རྣམ་རྟོག་སྐྱུར་ན་རྣམ་རྟོག་མང་དུ་འཕྲོ།།
བསྒོམ་པ་མ་སྐྱུར་རྣམ་རྟོག་ངོ་བོར་ལྟོས།།
སྐབས་རེར་ཡལ་ལ་སྐབས་རེ་འཕྲོ་བ་ལ།།
རྒྱུན་དུ་བསྒོམས་ན་རིམ་གྱིས་ཞི་བར་འགྲོ།།

nam tok kyur na nam tok mang du tro
gom pa ma kyur nam tok ngowor tö
kap rer yel la kap ré trowa la
gyün du gom na rim gyi zhiwar dro

If you try to get rid of thoughts, they will just increase. Instead, look at their essence, at their true face, without throwing away your meditation in the process.

At times thoughts vanish and at times they proliferate. If you meditate continually, they will gradually be pacified.

གོམས་ན་སྣ་བ་མ་ཡིན་པའི།།
བྱ་དངོས་ཅི་ཡང་ཡོད་མ་ཡིན།།
བསྒོམ་པ་མ་ཡིན་གོམས་པ་ཡིན།།
གོམས་པ་སློང་དུ་གྱུར་བ་ཡིན།།

gom na lawa ma yin pé
ja ngö chi yang yö ma yin
gom pa ma yin gom pa yin
gom pa long du gyur ba yin

Once you get used to it,
there is nothing difficult about it.
It is not meditation, it is just familiarizing.
It is completely mastering familiarization.

བདེ་སྐྱག་བར་གསུམ་ཆོར་བ་མང་པོ་དང་།།
བཟང་ངན་བར་གསུམ་རྣམ་རྟོག་ཅི་འཕྲོ་ཡང་།།
དགག་སྒྲུབ་སྤྱང་ལ་དྲན་པས་འཛིན་པར་བྱ།།
འགྱུ་བ་བྲི་ནས་གནས་པ་ཤས་ཆེར་འབྱུང་།།

dé duk bar sum tsorwa mang po dang
zang ngen bar sum nam tok chi tro yang
gak drup pang la dren pé dzin par ja
gyu ba dri né né pa shé cher jung

No matter what pleasant, unpleasant
and neutral feelings, and good, bad or neutral
thoughts multiply,
don't deny or affirm them, just hold them
mindfully. Once the movement of your thoughts
dies down, your mind will by and large come
to a state of rest.

སེམས་ཀྱི་རྣམ་རྟོག་ཞི་བར་གནས་གྱུར་ན།།
སེམས་ངོ་དྭངས་ལ་གསལ་བའི་རང་བཞིན་ཅན།།
ལུས་སེམས་བདེ་ལ་མི་རྟོག་གནས་ལུགས་འཆར།།
གནས་པ་སེམས་ཀྱི་བསྒོམ་བཞིན་གོམས་པར་གྱིས།།

sem kyi nam tok zhi bar né gyur na
sem ngo dang la selwé rang zhin chen
lü sem dé la mi tok né luk char
né pa sem kyi gom zhin gom par gyi

Once your thoughts have calmed down,
when your mind enters its resting state,
it possesses the very nature of clarity,
the pure lucidity of the essence of mind.
Body and mind are blissful and at ease,
and the non-conceptuality of the basic state

of being arises. Familiarize yourself with this
as you meditate on mind in its resting state.

སེམས་གནས་བརྟན་ལ་བདེ་གསལ་མི་རྟོག་པ།།
རྩོལ་མེད་འཆར་ལ་ནན་བསྒོམ་ཡོངས་བའི་དུས།།
རྣམ་རྟོག་ཤར་ཡང་དྲན་པས་འཛིན་ཐུབ་ན།།
སེམས་གནས་མཉམ་བཞག་བརྟན་པ་ཐོབ་པ་ཡིན།།

sem né ten la dé sel mi tok pa
tsöl mé char la nam gom yongwé dü
nam tok shar yang dren pé dzin tup na
sem né nyam zhak ten pa top pa yin

With stability in this mental abiding,
non-conceptual bliss-and-clarity
appear without effort. If, when the time comes
to meditate, you can catch your thoughts by
becoming mindful of them as they appear,
then you have gained confidence and stability
in the resting state and in mental equanimity.

རྣམ་རྟོག་ཀྲོད་ལ་ཉིན་མོངས་རགས་གྱུར་ནས།།
ཆེས་ཀྱང་མི་ཁོག་རྟོག་ཚོགས་འཕོ་གྱུར་ན།།
གང་འདོད་བཏང་ལ་དེ་ཡི་རོ་བོར་ལྷོས།།
ཡང་ན་ཕུག་སོར་རྣུང་སློར་ཁམས་གསེང་བྱ།།

nam tok gö la nyön mong rak gyur né
chi kyang mi khok tok tsok tro gyur na
gang dö tang la dé yi ngowor tö
yang na chak kor lung jor kham seng ja

When your mind becomes wild and gets all
agitated by thoughts; when it is filled with rough,
afflictive emotions, and abounds with thoughts
which are impossible to stop in any way.
Just let them be free, let them go as they please
and watch their nature.
Alternatively, [if this mind method does not work
then] do prostrations, circumabulations, yogic
breath-and-energy exercises or just take a break
from practice.

Part II

Meditating on the Mind-in-Motion

གཉིས་པ། སེམས་འགྱུ་བའི་བསྒོམ།

མ་བཏང་ན་ཡང་གར་དུ་འགྲོ་བ་དང་།།
མ་བཟུམ་ན་ཡང་རང་གིས་བཟུམ་པ་དང་།།
མ་བསྐུལ་ན་ཡང་གཡོ་ཞིང་འགྱུ་བ་དེའི།།
ངོ་བོ་ཅེར་གྱིས་ལྟོས་ལ་ཕྱམ་མེར་ཞོག།

ma tang na yang gang dundro ba dang
ma dam na yang rang gi dam pa dang
ma gül na yang yo zhing gyu ba dé
ngowo cher gyi tö la cham mer zhok

Even if you don't let thoughts go,
they go anyway.
Even if you don't hold onto them,
they cling to you anyway.
Even if you don't incite them,
they move around and are agitated anyway.
Whatever they do, look directly at their essence
and just leave them as they are.

ཚོལ་མེད་འཆར་ཞིང་རྣམ་པར་གཡེང་བ་དང་།།
འཛིན་མེད་འཆོར་ཞིང་སྨིག་རྒྱུ་ལྟ་བུར་གཡོ།།
བཟང་དང་དན་དང་ལུང་དུ་མ་བསྟན་རིགས།།
ཆད་མེད་འགྱུ་བའི་ངོ་བོར་ཡང་ཡང་ལྟོས།།

tsöl mé char zhing nam par yengwa dang
dzin mé chor zhing mik gyu ta bur yo
zang dang ngen dang lung du ma ten rik
ché mé gyu bé ngowor yang yang tö

When thoughts appear without you even trying
and completely distract you,
and when they lead astray you like a thick fog
and you lose your non-grasping,
no matter whether they are good, bad,
or neutral kinds of thoughts,
just continually keep looking at their nature,
at the essence of their movement.

རྣམ་རྟོག་ཇི་པ་ལྟ་བུར་འཁྱམ་པ་དེ།།
དྲན་ཤེས་ཨ་མ་ལྟ་བུས་ཡང་ཡང་བཟྲི།།
ཇི་པ་ཚེ་ཆིང་རྒྱུག་འདུར་ཅི་བྱ་ཡང་།།
ཐང་ཆད་མ་པང་ལོག་ལྟར་རིག་པར་ཐིམ།།

nam tok ji pa ta bur khyam pa dé
dren shé a ma ta bü yang yang dzi
ji pa tsé ching gyuk dur chi ja yang
tang ché ma pang lok tar rik par tim

78

Your thoughts are like a child that wanders off, and your mindful awareness is like their loving mother that shepherds them back again and again. However much the child exerts itself and runs away, it returns, exhausted, to its mother's lap. Like this, your thoughts dissolve into pure awareness.

རྣམ་རྟོག་མ་འགོག་རྣམ་རྟོག་སྐྱེ་རུ་ཆུག།
རྣམ་རྟོག་རྗེས་འདེད་མགོ་ང་གང་རུང་འཇུ།།
དེ་ནས་རྣམ་རྟོག་རོ་བོར་ཅེར་གྱིས་ལྟོས།།
སྟོང་སངས་མེད་ན་རྣམ་རྟོག་རང་གྲོལ་ཡིན།།

nam tok ma gok nam tok kyé ru chuk
nam tok jé dé go nga gang rung ju
dé né nam tok ngowor cher gyi tö
tong sang mé na nam tok rang dröl yin

Don't block conceptual thoughts, let them arise.
Pursue them and grab them by head or tail
And then look at their bare nature directly.
This is the totally transparent emptiness and purity of the essence of mind, or the spontaneous and automatic 'self-liberation' of thoughts.

འདས་དོན་མ་བརྗེད་ཡང་ཡང་དྲན་དུ་ཆུག །
དྲན་དུ་ཆུག་ལ་མགོ་ང་གང་རུང་བཟུང་། །
དེ་ནས་དྲན་པའི་རོ་བོར་ཆེར་གྱིས་ལྟོས། །
སྟོང་སངས་མེད་ན་དྲན་པ་རང་གྲོལ་ཡིན། །

dé dön ma jé yang yang dren du chuk
dren du chuk la go nga gang rung zung
dé né dren pé ngowor cher gyi tö
tong sang mé na dren pa rang dröl yin

Don't forget all the things that happened in
the past – recall them again and again!
Being mindful, seize your memories by head
or tail. Then look at the naked essence of your
memories directly. This is the totally transparent
emptiness and purity, the self-liberation of
memories.

ཞེ་སྡང་མ་འགོག་ཞེ་སྡང་ལངས་ཀྱི་ཆུག །
ཞེ་སྡང་བཟུང་ལ་རོ་བོར་ཆེར་གྱིས་ལྟོས། །
ཞེ་སྡང་ཁོང་ཁྲོ་སྟོང་སངས་མེད་གྱུར་ན། །
གསལ་སྟོང་དབྱེར་མེད་རིག་པ་རང་གྲོལ་ཡིན། །

zhé dang ma gok zhé dang lang kyi chuk
zhé dang zung la ngowor cher gyi tö
zhé dang khong tro tong sang mé gyur na
sel tong yer mé rik pa rang dröl yin

Don't block your hatred or aggression,
let it unfold.
Apprehend it and look directly at its nature.
When your hatred and anger is transformed
into indivisible emptiness-and-purity,
then this is the inseparability
of clarity-emptiness, the self-liberation
of natural awareness.

འདོད་ཆགས་མ་སྤངས་འདོད་ཆགས་མང་པོ་བསྒོམས།།
འདོད་པ་ཤར་དུས་འདོད་པའི་རོ་བོར་ལྟོས།།
ཡུལ་ལ་འཛིན་ཞིང་ཆགས་པའི་སེམས་ལ་དཔྱོད།།
བདེ་གསལ་སྟོང་བར་མཐོང་ན་རང་གྲོལ་ཡིན།།

dö chak ma pang dö chak mang po gom
dö pa shar dü dö pé ngowor tö
yül la dzin zhing chak pé sem la chö
dé sel tong bar tong na rang dröl yin

Don't renounce your desire,
cultivate it increasingly.
When desire arises, look at its nature.
Investigate the object of your desire
and the kind of mind which gives rise to it.
When you perceive desire and clarity as empty,
this is the self-liberation of desire.

ང་རྒྱལ་མ་འགོག་ང་རྒྱལ་སྐྱེ་རུ་ཆུག །
ང་རྒྱལ་སྐྱེ་བའི་ཁུངས་དང་གནས་པའི་ཡུལ། །
ཐ་མར་གང་འགྲོ་ཡང་ཡང་བཙལ་བར་བྱ། །
གསལ་ལ་སྟོང་པའི་ངོ་བོ་མཐོང་བར་བསྒོམ། །

nga gyel ma gok nga gyel kyé ru chuk
nga gyel kyewé khung dang né pé yül
ta mar gang dro yang yang tselwar ja
sel la tong pé ngowo tongwar gom

Don't block your pride, let it arise.
Again and again look into the origin of your
pride, into the depths of its arising and the
object(s) through which it endures.
Wherever you end up, look for these things
again and again, and meditate to perceive
their clear-and-empty nature.

ཕྲག་དོག་མ་སྤང་ཕྲག་དོག་ལངས་ཀྱི་ཆུག །
ཕྲག་དོག་སྐྱེ་བའི་ཁུངས་དང་གནས་པའི་ཡུལ། །
ཐ་མར་གང་འགྲོ་ཡང་ཡང་བཙལ་བར་བྱ། །
གསལ་ལ་སྟོང་པའི་ངོ་བོ་མཐོང་བར་བསྒོམ། །

trak dok ma pang trak dok lang kyi chuk
trak dok kyewé khung dang né pé yül
ta mar gang dro yang yang tselwar ja
sel la tong pé ngowo tongwar gom

Don't renounce your jealousy, let it come forth.
Look again and again into the depths of its
arising and the objects through which it abides.
Wherever you end up going, look for these things
again and again, and meditate to perceive their
clear-and-empty essence.

ཞེད་དངངས་མ་འགོག་འཇིགས་སྐྲག་སྐྱེ་རུ་ཆུག།
སྤང་ཐབས་མི་བྱ་དངངས་སྐྲག་ངོ་བོར་ལྟོས།།
སྟོང་སངས་རེག་འཛིན་མེད་ན་རང་གྲོལ་ཡིན།།
མ་ཡེང་གསལ་སྟོང་ཀློང་དུ་རིག་པ་སྐྱོངས།།

zhé ngang ma gok jik trak kyé ru chuk
pang tap mi ja ngang trak ngowor tö
tong sang rek dzin mé na rang dröl yin
ma yeng sel tong long du rik pa kyong

Don't block your fear, let your terror arise.
Without trying to do anything to rid yourself
of your fear, look at the essence of your terror.
This is the total emptiness and purity that cannot
be touched or grasped, the self-liberation of fear.
Without getting distracted maintain awareness in
the expanse of clarity-emptiness.

དོགས་པ་མ་སྤང་དོགས་པ་འདྲ་མིན་སྤེལ།།
དོགས་པ་ཤར་དུས་དེ་ཡི་ངོ་བོར་ལྟོས།།
དོགས་པ་འཛིན་མེད་སྟོང་པར་མཐོང་གྱུར་ན།།
ཤར་གྲོལ་ངོ་བོ་ཡིན་པས་ཡང་ཡང་སྐྱོངས།།

dok pa ma pang dok pa dra min pel
dok pa shar dü dé yi ngowor tö
dok pa dzin mé tong par tong gyur na
shar dröl ngowo yin pé yang yang kyong

Don't renounce your doubts, instead increase
all sorts of different misgivings.
When apprehensions and doubts appear,
look at their nature.
When you perceive your suspicions as empty
and devoid of any object to grasp onto,
this is the essence of liberating whatever arises
– so nurture it again and again!

སེམས་ཁྲལ་མ་སྤང་སེམས་ཁྲལ་དྲན་ཤེས་བསྟེན།།
དེ་ཡི་ཕྱི་རོལ་རྒྱུ་རྐྱེན་མ་བསམས་པར།།
ནང་གི་མི་སྐྱིད་སེམས་ཁྲལ་ངོ་བོར་ལྟོས།།
བརྟགས་ཀྱིན་མེད་པར་སངས་ན་རང་གྲོལ་ཡིན།།

sem trel ma pang sem trel dren shé ten
dé yi chi röl gyu kyen ma sam par
nang gi mi kyi sem trel ngowor tö
té kyin mé par sang na rang dröl yin

Without rejecting your worrying, be firmly
mindful of it. Without thinking about outside
causes or conditions of your worries,
look at the essence of your inner unhappy state
of worry. If this state clears away completely as
you look at it, then that's its self-liberation!

སྐྱོ་བའི་དུས་སུ་སྐྱོ་བའི་ངོ་བོར་ལྟོས།།
དགའ་བའི་དུས་སུ་དགའ་བའི་ངོ་བོར་ལྟོས།།
བདེ་སྡུག་བཟང་ངན་ཡིད་ཀྱི་ལྐོག་བརྙན་ལ།།
ཡང་ཡང་ལྟོས་དང་སྒྱུ་འཕྲུལ་རང་གྲོལ་ཡིན།།

kyowé dü su kyowé ngowor tö
gawé dü su gawé ngowor tö
dé duk zang ngen yi kyi lok nyen la
yang yang tö dang gyuntrül rang dröl yin

When you are sad, look at the essence
of your sadness. When you are happy look
at the essence of your happiness.
Look again and again at the pleasurable
and painful, good and bad movies of your mind
– this is the self-liberation of the mind's illusions,
of all of its glamorous projections!

Part III

Meditating on Rigpa, Natural Awareness

གསུམ་པ། རིག་པའི་བསྒོམ།

དང་པོ་གནས་པའི་སེམས་དེ་བརྟན་པ་དང་། །
བར་དུ་གཡོ་བའི་སེམས་ངོ་དྲན་པས་འཛིན། །
ཐ་མར་གསལ་སྟོང་རིག་ངོ་མཐོང་བ་ནི། །
རྫོགས་ཆེན་ཁྲེགས་ཆོད་གནས་ལུགས་འཁྲུལ་མེད་ཡིན། །

dang po né pé sem dé ten pa dang
bar du yowé sem ngo dren pé dzin
ta mar sel tong rik ngo tongwa ni
dzok chen trek chö né luk trül mé yin

First, you stabilize the mind in its resting state,
then as the middle step, you stay mindful of
the essence of your thoughts-in-motion.
Finally, you perceive clarity-emptiness, which
is the essence of pure and natural awareness.
This is the Great Perfection, the Cutting Through
Hardness to the state of things as they are,
without delusion.

གནས་དུས་ཞི་ལ་འགྱུ་དུས་གསལ་བ་དང་།།
སྣང་བ་ཕྱི་མིན་སེམས་དེ་ནང་མ་ལུས།།
རིག་པ་ཟངས་ཐལ་སོ་སོ་མ་ཡིན་པར།།
འཛིན་མེད་བསྒོམ་མེད་བསྒོམ་པའི་མཁན་པོ་བྲལ།།

né dü zhi la gyu dü selwa dang
nangwa chi min sem dé nang ma lü
rik pa zang tel so so ma yin par
dzin mé gom mé gom pé khen po drel

When mind is at rest it is peaceful,
when mind is in motion it is clear.
Its displays are not external but are entirely
within the mind. Natural awareness is completely
transparent – it is completely undivided,
it is not a 'thing' you can grasp, it cannot be
cultivated through meditation, it is free from
any 'meditator'.

སྟོང་བས་སྣང་བ་སྒྲིབ་པར་མི་བྱེད་ལ།།
སྣང་བས་སྟོང་བ་འགོག་པར་མི་བྱེད་པ།།
སྣང་སྟོང་འགལ་མེད་དབྱེར་མེད་ཆེན་པོ་དེ།།
རིག་པའི་ངོ་བོ་རང་ཤར་རང་གྲོལ་སྐྱོངས།།

tong bé nangwa drip par mi jé la
nangwé tong ba gok par mi jé pa
nang tong gel mé yer mé chen po dé
rik pé ngowo rang shar rang dröl kyongg

The essence of natural awareness appears
and is liberated into emptiness entirely
of its own accord.
Its emptiness aspect is not obscured
by mental appearances or visions,
and its visionary aspect doesn't block
its innate emptiness.
In it appearances-and-emptiness are totally
united without any contradiction. Nurture it!

ཡོད་པ་མ་ཡིན་རྒྱལ་བས་གཟིགས་མ་ཡིན།།
མེད་པ་མ་ཡིན་འཁོར་འདས་ཀུན་ལ་ཁྱབ།།
གསལ་སྟོང་བདེ་སྟོང་རིག་སྟོང་བདག་ཉིད་ཅན།།
གཟུགས་ཅན་གཟུགས་མེད་ལས་འདས་ཨེ་མ་ཧོ།།

yö pa ma yin gyelwé zik ma yin
mé pa ma yin khor dé kün la khyap
sel tong dé tong rik tong dak nyi chen
zuk chen zuk mé lé dé é ma ho

It is not something existent, it is unseen even
by Buddhas. Yet it is not non-existent, since it
pervades all of Samsara-and-Nirvana.
It is the personification of clarity-emptiness,
bliss-emptiness, awareness-emptiness.
It is beyond all form and formlessness
– Wow! So amazing!

སེམས་ངོ་འཕྲོད་ནས་རིག་པ་ཁོ་ན་སྐྱོངས།།
གནས་དང་དུས་ལ་ཁྱད་མེད་ལམ་འཁྱེར་བྱོས།།
དུག་ལྔ་རང་གྲོལ་ཚོགས་དྲུག་རང་གྲོལ་འདི།།
རིག་པ་ཁོ་ནར་ཐག་ཆོད་གོལ་ས་མེད།།

sem ngo trö né rik pa kho na kyong
né dang dü la khyé mé lam khyer jö
duk nga rang dröl tsok druk rang dröl di
rik pa kho nar tak chö göl sa mé

Once you've understood natural awareness,
nurture it and nothing else.
Bring your emotions and experiences
'onto the path'; bring them into your practice
no matter the time or place.
Confirm this self-liberation of the 'five poisons'
or afflictive emotions and of the 'six collections'
or the modes of consciousness for yourself.
Confirm natural awareness and natural awareness
alone, without getting sidetracked!

ལྷ་ལ་རེ་བ་འདྲེ་ལ་མི་དོགས་པ།།
འཚོ་དུས་བདེ་ལ་འཆི་ཀ་འོད་གསལ་རིག།
ཨ་ཏིའི་གདིང་ཆེན་ཐོབ་པའི་དུན་རྒྱགས་དང་།།
ཚེ་འདིར་བཅའན་ས་རང་ས་ཟིན་པ་འོ།།

lha la rewa dré la mi dok pa
tso dü dé la chi ka ö sel rik

a ti ding chen top pé den tak dang
tsé dir tsen sa rang sa zin pao

Not placing your hopes in the deities
or fearing demons, being full of joy while alive
and recognizing the Clear Light Awareness at the
moment of death – this is proof that you have
obtained the profundity of Ati Yoga,
that you have seized the stronghold of
Dharmakaya, the absolute reality, that you have
grasped firmly your own innate state.

དགའ་བཞིའི་ཐིག་ལེའི་ལྷུན་སྐྱེས་འོད་གསལ་དང་།།
ཡེ་ཤེས་རླུང་སྦྱོར་ཡང་དག་སྒྱུ་ལུས་ཀྱང་།།
མ་རིག་མུན་བྲལ་རིག་པའི་ཀློང་དུ་འཆར།།
འཇའ་ལུས་འཕོ་བ་ཆེན་པོ་མངོན་འགྱུར་ཤོག།།

ga zhi tik lé lhen kyé ö sel dang
yé shé lung jor yang dak gyu lü kyang
ma rik mün drel rik pé long du char
ja lü powa chen po ngön gyur shok

The co-emergent Light and Clarity of the energy
drops of the four blisses, the Primordial Wisdom
that comes from the uniting of the winds, the
totally pure illusory body – all of these arise from
the expanse of natural awareness that is free from
the darkness of non-awareness. May the great
transference of the rainbow body manifest!

སྔགས་སྐྱོན་ཅེ་རླུང་བླ་མ་གོང་མའི་གསུང་དང་རང་གི་ཉམས་མྱོང་ལྷར་རྣལ་འབྱོར་ཕོ་མོ་བློ་གསར་རྣམས་ཀྱི་སེམས་ངོ་བསྐྱང་བར་ཕུར་ཚམ་ཕན་ན་བསམ་ནས་ནས། གཡུ་ཐོག་རྫོགས་ཆེན་འཁོར་འདས་རང་གྲོལ་གྱི་ཆ་ལག་ཏུ་༢༠༡༧-༡-༡༦ ཉིན་ཀྱི་ཡོ་ཏོ་ Kyoto ནས་བྲིས་པའོ།།

Drawing from the teachings of previous gurus and his own personal experience, the crazy yogi Nida wrote this on the 16th of January 2017 in Kyoto as a supplementary instruction on *Yuthok's Great Perfection Self-Liberation of Samsara -Nirvana*, thinking that it might help newbie yogis and yoginis just a little with nurturing and maintaining recognition of their minds' true essence.

This text is dedicated to:
མོན་མོ་བཀྲ་ཤིས་སྒྲི་འཛིན།
Khandroma Mönmo Tashi Chidren
མཁའ་འགྲོ་ཚེ་རིང་ཆོས་སྒྲོན།
Khandro Tshering Chödron

Mönmo's Ati Yoga

གུ་རུ་རིན་པོ་ཆེས་མོན་མོ་བཀྲ་ཤིས་སྒྲི་འབྲེན་
ལ་གནང་བའི་སེམས་ཁྲིད།

Guru Rinpoche's Teaching on Mind
Given to Lady Tashi Chidren of Mönmo
(Revealed by Terton Guru Chöwang)

མ་ཧཱ་གུ་རུ་པདྨ་ལ༔ བཀྲ་ཤིས་འབྲེན་གྱིས་ཡང་གསོལ་པ༔ རྗེ་མོའི་
གསང་སྒྲུབ་གསུང་བར་ཞུ༔ མ་ཧཱ་གུ་རུས་བཀའ་བསྩལ་པ༔ དགེ་
ལྡན་སེམས་མ་ཡང་ཉིད་ཅིག༔ མ་གཅིག་རྗེ་མོ་མཚོ་རྒྱལ་ནི༔ གསང་
བར་མ་མོ་བདག་མེད་མ༔ འཁོར་བ་བློས་བཏང་གངས་ཕུག་གི་ཏེ་རི་
ཁྲོད་དབེན་སར་འཁོལ་གནེན་སྲིང༔ གསང་སྔགས་བླ་མ་བཟང་བཞིན་
ནས༔ གཅུག་གི་རྒྱན་གཅིག་བདག་མེད་མ༔ རང་རང་གཉིས་མེད་
བསླ་འདོད་ནུ༔ འདི་ལྟར་བདག་ལ་གཞིག་པ་བཏང༔

And again, Tashi (Chi)dren asked the great
Lotus Guru – Pray, teach the Secret (Guru Yoga)
Sadhana of the Venerable Lady Yeshe Tsogyal!

The Great Guru gave these instructions:

"Listen, virtuous Bodhisattva! The secret
aspect of the sole mother Lady Tsogyal is
Mamo Dakmema, the No-Self Mamo or Mother
Goddess! Having abandoned samsara, atop a
cushion in a secluded place of retreat amidst
snowy peaks, commit yourself properly to her,
your Secret Mantra guru. If you want to observe
your nonduality, your ultimate oneness with her,
the No-Self Lady Yeshe Tsogyal who is the sole
ornament that crowns your head, then investigate
your 'self', like this:

ཕྱི་ནང་ཡུལ་ལ་བདག་ཚོལ་ཅིག། སྣང་ཡུལ་སེམས་ལ་ཕར་བརྟགས་
པས། སྣང་བའི་ཡུལ་ལ་བདག་མེད་ནུ། མིང་རུས་བདག་ཏུ་འདུག
གམ་ལྟོས། མིང་དང་རུས་ནི་བདག་ཡིན་ནུ། མིང་རུས་འགོ་ཚོ་བདག
མི་འགོ། དེ་ཕྱིར་མིང་རུས་བདག་མ་ཡིན། ལུས་འདི་བདག་ཏུ་འདུག
གམ་ལྟོས། ལུས་འདི་བདག་ཉིད་ཡིན་གྱུར་ནུ། ལུས་འདི་བཤིགས་
ཚེ་བདག་མི་ཚིག། ཕྱི་ཡི་ལུས་ནི་བདག་མ་ཡིན། ནོ་ན་སེམས་ནི་
བདག་ཡིན་ནམ། སེམས་འདི་བདག་གཅིག་ཡིན་གྱུར་ནུ། ད་ལྟ་གར་
གནས་དང་པོ་གང་ནས་བྱུང་། རྗེས་ལ་གར་འགྲོ་དཔྱིབས་དང་ཁ་དོག་
ལྟོས། གང་དུ་ཡང་ནི་གྲུབ་པ་མེད་

Look for your 'self', for an 'I' in external and
internal objects. If, examining appearances out
there with the mind, you discover that they lack

any concrete self, look at your personal and family names – are they the self? If they were, then if one's names changed then the self too would change. Yet it does not, so the self is not one's personal or family titles. Then look: is the self this body of yours? If this body of yours were your ultimate self then when it was cremated then the self would burn up as well. Yet it does not, and so the external body is not the self. So then, is the mind the self? If it is so that the mind is the sole self then look (to see if you can discover) where your present mind came from, where will it go to later, what is its shape, its color? Whatever and wherever your mind is, it is not made up of anything – it has no concrete existence at all.

སེམས་ནི་སྐྱོང་པ་སྐྱེ་འགགས་མེད༔ དེ་ཕྱིར་སེམས་ལ་དང་བདག །
མེད༔ གཞན་ནའང་ཡོད་པ་མ་ཡིན་ཏེ༔ དེ་ལྟར་ལྟ་བྱེད་བདག་མ་
ཡིན༔ ཅི་སྟེ་རང་བཞིན་བརྟོད་དང་བྲལ༔ བདག་མེད་པ་ལ་བདག །
བཟུང་བས༔ སེམས་ཅན་ཐམས་ཅད་འཁྲུལ་ཅིང་སྲུག །ཉིན་མོངས་
བཀྱུད་ཁྲི་བཞི་སྟོང་ཡང༔ རྩ་བ་བདག་ཏུ་རྟོག་ལས་གྱེས༔ བདག་མེད་
རང་རིག་དེ་རྟོགས་ན༔ སངས་རྒྱས་བྱང་ཆུབ་བདེ་བ་རྒྱས༔ ཆོས་སྐྱེ་
བཀྱུད་ཁྲི་བཞི་སྟོང་ཡང༔ བདག་མེད་ཟབ་སར་སྒྲོལ་ལ་འདུས༔ དེ་
ཕྱིར་མ་མོ་བདག་མེད་མ༔ མ་ནི་སྐྱེ་བ་མེད་པའི་དོན༔ མོ་ནི་འགགས་
པ་མེད་པའི་དོན༔ བདག་མེད་སྐྱེ་འགགས་གཉིས་ལས་འདས༔ དེ་ལྟར་
རྟོགས་ན་ལྷ་བ་ཡིན༔ རང་རིག་བདག་མེད་གསལ་བ་དེ༔ མ་ཡེངས་
རྒྱུན་དུ་སྒོམ་པ་ཡིན༔ དེ་ལས་མི་འདའ་དམ་ཚིག་ཡིན༔ ཡིད་ལ་མི་
བྱེད་གེགས་སེལ་ཡིན༔ དེ་བཞིན་སྤྱད་པ་སྒྲོད་པ་ཡིན༔ དེ་དོན་མངོན་
གྱུར་འབྲས་བུ་ཡིན༔

The mind is unborn and unending – because of this, it has no self, no 'I', nor is it any other thing that exists. It is likewise not the self who observes. It is devoid of any nature that can be expressed. Even though the mind has no self, by holding on to the idea of one all beings are deluded and suffer. All 84,000 mental afflictions radiate out from the root of the concept of an 'I'. If you realize selfless self-awareness, the bliss of the 'extensive clearing away of all impurity, of total mastery and realization' (i.e. Buddhahood) will bloom. All the 84,000 different teachings or 'doorways to the Dharma' lead to the same conclusion of no-self! The *'ma'* in Mamo Dakmema signifies the bornlessness of mind, the *'mo'* signifies its unceasingness. Selflessness transcends both birth and death, both arising and passing away. If you realize that, then that's the View (ལྟ་བ། *lta ba*). Meditation or 'familiarizing' (བསྒོམ་པ། *bsgom pa*) means continually cultivating the clear and spontaneous, innate self-awareness of non-self without distraction. Never straying from that is the tantric Vow or Pledge (དམ་ཚིག། *dam tshig*). Not succumbing to conceptuality, the mind not fabricating anything – that is the Resolving of Hindrances (གེགས་སེལ། *gegs sel*). To act thus is the Conduct (སྤྱོད་པ། *spyod pa*). To make manifest (the mind's own nature) as described above is the Fruit or Result (འབྲེས་བུ། *'bres bu*).

འབྱུངཿ འགྲོ་དོན་ལྷུན་གྲུབ་ཆེན་པོར་སྐྱོངཿ འདི་ལྷ་བུ་ཡི་རིན་ཆེན་ འདིཿ བློ་དམན་རྣམས་ལ་གསང་བའི་དོནཿ སྒྱལ་ལྡན་འདི་སྤྱོད་གསང་ སྒྲུབ་ཅེསཿ ཐ་སྙད་ཚམ་དུ་བཏགས་པ་བསཿ དེ་ཕྱིར་གསང་སྒྲུབ་འདི་ ལྷར་རྟོགསཿ བཀྲ་ཤིས་འཛིན་ཁྱོད་སྐལ་ལྡན་ནམཿ གཙུག་གི་རྒྱན་ གཅིག་རྣལ་འབྱོར་མཿ བདག་མེད་པ་ཡི་དོན་རྟོགས་ཤོགཿ

This is the crowning summit of every vehicle
or spiritual path, it is the sole adornment that
goes beyond all pain and suffering, this great,
miraculous, all-liberating selflessness! Non-self is
the empowerment-possessing Dharmakaya, the
body of ultimate reality, which is clear and lucid
as the sky, and the two form-aspect bodies (i.e.
the Enjoyment and Emanation bodies) emerge
from it naturally and spontaneously, shining
forth like the rays of the sun. Accomplish this
greatness, which spontaneously realizes benefit
for all beings! This hugely precious truth is
something secret or hidden to those of lesser
capacity – so make use of it, o fortunate lady!
Realize this truth, that which is only conventionally
named the 'secret sadhana' (for it is beyond all
conceptual thought and labels). Aren't you lucky,
Tashi (Chi)dren? May you, the Yogini whose head
is crowned with no other ornament than her
Guru, realize this truth of selflessness!"

རྗེ་མོའི་གསང་སྒྲུབ་ཡང་དག་དོན་གྱི་ལེའུ་སྟེ་བཞི་པའོ༔…དཔེ་
གཅིག་ལ། རྩ་རིད་གཞིན་ནུའི་སྒྱུལ་པ་མོན་ཙནྡྲས་ཡི་གེར་བཏབ་
པའོ༔ མཆན། ས་མ་ཡཿ ཨི་ཐི༔ རྒྱ་རྒྱ་རྒྱ༔ གུ་རུ་ཆོས་ཀྱི་དབང་ཕྱུག་
གི་གཏེར་མའོ།། །།

'The Secret Sadhana of the Lady', which is the
fourth among the chapters on the authentic truth.
Written down by the emanation of 'The Youthful
Moonlight', Mön Chandra.

CHEN SAMAYA ITA GYA GYA GYA!
Bound and sealed!

From the treasure of Guru Chöwang

The Five Line Prayer to Yuthok

དུས་གསུམ་རྒྱལ་ཀུན་གསང་བ་གཅིག་བསྡུས་པ།།

Dü sum gyel kün sangwa chik dü pa

To the secret union of all buddhas
of the three times,

བླ་མ་སྨན་པའི་རྒྱལ་པོ་གཡུ་ཐོག་པར།།

La ma men pe gyel po yu tok par

To the Guru Yuthok, the King of Medicine,

སྙིང་ཁོང་རུས་པའི་གཏིང་ནས་གསོལ་བ་འདེབས།།

Nying khong rü pe ting ne sölwa dep

I pray from the depths of my heart and bones:

སྐུ་གསུང་ཐུགས་ཀྱི་བྱིན་གྱིས་རློབ་པ་དང་།།

Ku sung tuk kyi jin gyi lop pa dang

Bless me through your body, speech, and mind,

མཆོག་དང་ཐུན་མོང་དངོས་གྲུབ་རྩལ་དུ་གསོལ།།

Chok dang tün mong ngö drup tsel du söl

Grant me the supreme and common siddhis.

གོང་སྤྲུལ་ནས།

By Kongtrul

BIBLIOGRAPHY

Tibetan Sources:

Chos kyi dbang phyug.
d+h Aki gtsug gi rgyan gcig ye shes mtsho rgyal gyi sgrub. From the Bla ma gsang ba 'dus pa treasure cycle, vol. 34, pp. 553-568/folios 1a1 to 8b5. In the Shechen edition of the Rinchen Terdzö:
http://rtz.tsadra.org/index.php/Terdzo-NGI-039

G.yu thog yon tan mgon po. 2005.
G.yu thog snying thig (sngags mang dpe tshogs). Beijing: Mi rigs dpe skrun khang.

Zhabs dkar tshogs drug rang grol. 2002.
'Od gsal rdzogs pa chen po'i khregs chod lta ba'i glu dbyangs lam ma lus myur du bgrod pa'i rtsal ldan mkha' lding gshog rlabs. In "Rje Zhabs dkar tshogs drug rang grol gyi gsung 'bum." Zi ling: Mtsho sngon mi rigs dpe skrun khang, pp. 581-633.

English Sources:

Chenagtsang, Nida.
Mirror of Light: A Commentary on Yuthok's Ati Yoga, Volume One. Portland: SKY Press, 2016.

Chenagtsang, Nida.
Transcripts from oral teachings given on the *Mirror of Light* book tour, December 2016 in the United States.

GLOSSARY

Ani Ngawang Gyaltsen (ཨ་ནེ་ངག་དབང་རྒྱལ་མཚན། *a ne ngag dbang rgyal mtshan*) - The heart disciple of Ani Lochen from Shugseb Nunnery. She was Dr Nida's teacher and transmitted to him the teachings of Ati Yoga, Mahamudra, and the Six Yogas.

Anu Yoga - The 'Further' or 'pre-eminent' yoga, the middle of the three top-most 'Inner Yogas' in the nine-fold list of vehicles in the Nyingma school of Tibetan Buddhism as taught by Padmasambhava. Directly preceding Ati Yoga, this vehicle emphasizes practices of the Completion Stage of Highest Yoga Tantra, and focuses on the manipulation of the Channels, Winds, and Drops to produce an 'Illusory Body' of a Buddha. It is the antidote to desire.

Arising - Abiding - Going (Jung སྦྱོང༌། *byung* - Né གནས། *gnas* - Dro འགྲོ། *'gro*) - In Ati Yoga, one must investigate the arising, abiding, and going of thoughts and emotions until one determintes definitively that there is no source from which the thoughts arose, no place in which they currently abide, and no place to which they have gone once they are no longer in one's mind stream.

Ati Yoga - The 'extreme,' 'ultimate,' or 'supreme' yoga, the highest of the three Inner Yogas in the Nyingma system and antidote for ignorance. Synonymous with

Dzogchen, the Great Perfection, this vehicle focuses on the practitioner's already-perfected Buddha nature, and the methods for spontaneously and naturally realizing and abiding in it (See Dzogchen).

Bodhisattva - A realized being who has transcended the round of death, rebirth, sickness, aging and death (Samsara), who chooses to continue to be reborn and manifest in existence to help liberate beings.

Completion stage (Dzogrim རྫོགས་རིམ། *rdzogs rim*) - Refers to advanced tantric yoga practices in which practitioners actually experience themselves as the meditational deity and thereby strongly familiarize themselves with their own enlightened nature. Typically follows after Creation Stage procedures, and involves working with the channels, winds, and drops, where the winds are directed into the central channel and dissolve at the heart, causing the mind of Clear Light to manifest.

Creation Stage (Kyerim བསྐྱེད་རིམ། *bskyed rim*) - The phase of tantric meditation or yoga in which practitioners visualize themselves and all appearances as the meditational deity and their Mandala, retinues etc. The practice involves meditating on the emptiness of phenomena and promotes the realization of the innate purity of all perceptions.

Dakini (Khandro མཁའ་འགྲོ། *mkha 'gro*) - 'Sky-Goer' – A tantric goddess. At times beautiful and at times terrifying, she appears in both 'wordly' and 'wisdom' forms. Worldly Dakinis can refer to either unenlightened disembodied goddesses and embodied human yoginis or female spiritual consorts, whereas wisdom Dakinis can point to non-physical, enlightened goddesses and female Buddhas, as well as to a particular quality or activity of enlightened awareness, to the dynamic, creative, playful, revelatory, and metaphorically feminine dimensions of innate wisdom-consciousness. Human women given this title are understood to be physical embodiments or equivalents of spiritual Dakinis and their qualities.

Dharmakaya (Chöku ཆོས་སྐུ། *chos sku*) - In the context of the 'Three Bodies' doctrine of Mahayana and Vajrayana Buddhism refers to the cosmic 'truth body' of the Buddha. The ultimate, non-dual, omniscient and wholly pure and liberated reality from which all Buddhas and Buddha-activities ultimately emerge.

Dzogchen (རྫོགས་ཆེན། *rdzogs chen*) - The Tibetan name for Ati Yoga, short for Dzogpa Chenpo which means the 'Great Perfection' or 'Completion', and points to the fact that all beings are perfect as they are, lacking nothing.

Garab Dorje (དགའ་རབ་རྡོ་རྗེ། *dga rab rdo rje*) - The semi-mythical master considered to be the first human recipient of the teachings of Ati Yoga in the Nyingma school of Tibetan Buddhism.

Guru Yoga - The practice of devotion to one's guru or spiritual teacher and guide, in which one trains in seeing one's teacher as a Buddha. Practitioners recite the guru's mantra, receive the guru's blessing, and ultimately unite their own minds with the guru's enlightened being. Guru Yoga is a mechanism for realizing one's own intrinsic 'guru' or Buddha-nature. In the Yuthok Nyingthig system there are four Guru Yoga practices which are practiced after the Ngöndro preliminary practices: Outer, Inner, Secret and Concise Guru Yoga. The Outer Guru Yoga is the method for creating an unbreakable link with Yuthok and is considered a preliminary practice for Ati Yoga in this system.

Khandro Tshering Chödron (མཁའ་འགྲོ་ཚེ་རིང་ཆོས་སྒྲོན། mkha 'gro tshe ring chos sgron) - A hidden yogini reincarnation of Mönmo Tashi Chidren and one of the inspirations behind this work.

Loong (རླུང་། rlung) - Wind energy of which there is both both karmic winds and wisdom winds in the subtle body. The karmic winds run through the 72,000 channels while the wisdom winds are contained in the central channel. Through the practice of Ati Yoga, the karmic winds are brought into the central channel where they are transformed into wisdom wind giving rise to the nondual experience.

Mahamudra (Chakchen ཕྱག་ཆེན་ *phyag chen*, short for Chagya Chenpo) - The 'Great Seal' or Symbol. Mahamudra refers to the profound awareness in which everyday appearances and ultimate emptiness are inseparably united through resting in the basic uncontrived nature of mind. In Yuthok's system, a condensed form of Mahamudra instruction is taught on its own, as cognate with the Trekchöd aspect of Ati Yoga.

Maha Yoga - The 'Great' yoga, the first of the three top-most 'Inner Yogas' in the nine-fold list of vehicles in the Nyingma school of Tibetan Buddhism. Corresponds with the Creation Stage of Highest Yoga Tantra, in which practitioners visualize themselves as the deity in order to manifest one's body as that of the deity, one's speech as mantra, and one's mind as that of the deity, beyond dualism, as well as one's surroundings as the deity's Mandala. Meditation can be done on both the peaceful and wrathful deities, but especially when visualizing the wrathful deities, Maha Yoga is considered the antidote to anger.

Mantra (སྔགས། *sngags*) - A Sanskrit word meaning 'to protect the mind', Mantra refers to a spoken or mentally intoned esoteric formula in the form of one or more syllables in Sanskrit or some other sacred language. As 'words of truth' revealed by great realized sages and adepts, mantras generate beneficial powers and qualities, focus the mind, and protect it from samsaric distractions.

Meditation (Gompa བསྒོམ་པ། *bsgom pa*) -
'Familiarization,' 'to familiarize.' In the context of Ati
Yoga, the meditation is to familiarize oneself with the
pure fresh awareness which is one's basic state.

Mönmo Tashi Chidren (མོན་མོ་བཀྲ་ཤིས་སྤྱི་འདྲེན། *mon mo bkra
shis spyi 'dren*) - One of the five great spiritual consorts
of Padmasambhava and an important devotee of
Yeshe Tsogyal. Originally named Tashi Khyeudren,
she is described in some accounts as the daughter
of a Bhutanese king from Bumthang. At the age of
thirteen she came across Yeshe Tsogyal while the
latter was meditating in a cave in Bhutan and was so
struck by the great yogini that she became her life-long
disciple. Noticing that Tashi Khyeudren possessed all
the marks of a great dakini, Yeshe Tsogyal requested
that the king give the girl to her, after which her name
was changed to Tashi Chidren. Tashi Chidren travelled
with Yeshe Tsogyal to Tibet and met Padmasambhava,
who took her as his consort to perfect the Vajrakilaya
practices through which he ensured the flourishing of
the Buddhist teachings in Tibet. Padmasambhava gave
the Ati Yoga teachings found in this book when Tashi
Chidren asked him to transmit extremely subtle Guru
Yoga teachings relating to Yeshe Tsogyal to her.

Naljor (རྣལ་འབྱོར། *rnal 'byor*) - The Tibetan translation
of the Sanskrit word yoga, meaning to attain (jorwa)
the original, pure, primordial state (nalma). Yogic
practitioners are called Naljorwa (for men) and
Naljorma (for women).

Ngöndro (སྔོན་འགྲོ། *sngon 'gro*) - Preliminary contemplative, devotional and purifying practices undertaken as required preparation before one engages with more advanced tantric yoga sadhanas. The Common Preliminaries typically refer to contemplations on the 'Four Thoughts that Turn the Mind (i.e. away from Samsara)' meant to instill renunciation or disillusionment with Samsara. The Uncommon Preliminaries involve accumulating repetitions of practices aimed at purifying obscurations, generating merit, and removing obstacles. In the Yuthok Nyingthig tradition these practices include: Refuge; Bodhicitta; Four Immeasurables; Prostrations; Mandala Offerings; Circumambulations, Vajrasattva, and Kusali practice which are practiced in the context of a seven day retreat, recommended to be repeated regularly. The Yuthok Nyingthig adds to the Common and Uncommon preliminaries a third category of 'Routine' Ngondro which encompasses various forms of everyday compassionate action to be engaged in after retreat in order to bring the benefits of one's practice into the world.

Nirvana - Literally 'extinction', the unconditioned reality beyond all conditioned and impermanent phenomena of Samsara. The ultimate goal of the Buddhist path, where 'extinction'; refers to the final cessation of afflictive emotions and the actions, effects and pain generated by these. While Nirvana is often described as a final escape from suffering, karma and the endless round of rebirth, it is important to remember that Samsara and Nirvana are exactly alike in their absolute lack of any inherent substance or existence. Samsara-Nirvana (Khor-De) thus appear as an indivisible pair in Yuthok's Ati Yoga teachings – all of Samsara AND Nirvana are wholly encompassed by the yogic practitioner's own awareness and being. (See Samsara).

Padmasambhava (Pema Jungné པད་འབྱུང་གནས། *pad ma 'byung gnas*) - Also called Guru Rinpoche or the 'Precious Guru', the great realized tantric master or Ngakpa from Oddiyana who is thought of by Tibetans as a 'Second Buddha'. He is credited with firmly establishing Buddhism in Tibet in the 8th century by calling forth and taming all of the indigenous pre-Buddhist land-spirits of Tibet, and redirecting their energies towards the flourishing of the Dharma. Guru Rinpoche is also the originator of the Terma or 'Treasure' tradition and founder of the Nyingma ('old') school of Vajrayana Buddhism.

Rainbow Body (Jalü འཇའ་ལུས། *'ja lus*) - As a result of practicing Dzogchen/Ati Yoga, and Togal in particular, advanced practitioners may achieve the so-called 'rainbow body' in which all or most of their physical body dissolves into multi-colored light at the time of death. Degrees of rainbow body exist – adepts may completely dissolve leaving no material trace behind, may leave nothing but fingernails and hair, or may exhibit a 'lesser transference rainbow body' in which their physical form dramatically and progressively shrinks over the course of about one week until it is the size of a small child.

Rigpa (རིག་པ། *rig pa*) - Pure awareness, referring to the basic nature of mind as it is, mind's wholly uncontrived wisdom or intelligence. It is the source of all Samsara-Nirvana. As the typically unrecognized basis of all experience, Rigpa contrasts with the Clear Light Mind in that it is not only accessible through induced states of extremely subtle consciousness, but is an all pervasive background reality, an already perfect, uncreated, spontaneous and natural awareness that can potentially be pointed out, recognized and stabilized at any moment.

Samaya (Damtsik དམ་ཚིག། *dam tshigs*) - A 'binding' or 'pure' pledge, the term used to denote a tantric vow or ritual commitment. In Vajrayana there are fourteen root tantric vows and eight 'thick' actions or secondary vows (although additional vows exist), which are presented in the form of behavior that the tantric practitioner ought to refrain from. Samaya vows are designed to create the perfect context for the practice of Guru Yoga and Highest Yoga Tantra, and are said to endure and to connect gurus and disciples across lifetimes.

Samsara - Literally 'Wandering/Circling around and around'. The state of conditioned existence, of continual rebirth and suffering. (See Nirvana)

Shabkar Tsokdruk Rangdrol (ཞབས་དཀར་ཚོགས་དྲུག་རང་གྲོལ། *zhabs dkar tshogs trug rang grol*, 1781-1851) - 'He of the White Feet, Self-Liberation of the Six Collections'.

A prominent Ati Yoga master, Ngakpa, and celebrated poet who was born in Amdo, Eastern Tibet. He wrote a number of highly influential commentaries on Ati Yoga, perhaps the most famous of which is his 'Flight of the Garuda'. He lived for many years as an itinerant yogi-meditator and contributed significantly to the preservation and development of the Ngakpa tradition.

Shamatha (Shinay ཞི་གནས། *zhi gnas*) - Translated as 'Peaceful Abiding' in Tibetan, Shamata refers to Buddhist methods for the cultivation of mental peace, concentration and stability. Shamatha together with Vipashyana, forms the backbone of Buddhist contemplative practice (See Vipashyana).

Terma (གཏེར་མ། *gter ma*) - 'Treasure' tradition originating with Padmasambhava where teachings and blessings in the form of physical objects and texts, as well as more immaterial transmissions were hidden in the sky, under the earth, in rocks and caves, and in the mind-streams of Guru Rinpoche's closest disciples so as to be uncovered and disseminated by future incarnations in later lifetimes. A tertön is a a revealer of these treasures.

Training (Jang སྦྱང་། *sbyang*) - In Tibetan, the word for training also means 'to purify.' Particular practices are done in order to training and purify the body, speech (energy) and mind as laid out in this text.

Trekchöd (ཁྲེགས་ཆོད། *khregs chod*) - 'cutting (chöd) through hardness (trek)' of dualistic appearances and our firm attachment to the misperception of things and thoughts as having innate substance. It is a method for revealing the basic purity of the mind, unadulterated by dualistic thinking.

Tögal (ཐོད་རྒལ། *thod rgal*) - 'Crossing', 'Leaping', or 'Skipping Over', also sometimes translated as 'Traversing the Skull'. The name given to advanced Ati Yoga practices which involve inducing intense visionary experiences as part of recognizing the luminous nature of all perceived phenomena. Tögal practices are connected with the eyes, visual perception, and special subtle light channels, and form a complement to Trekchöd. While Trekchöd emphasizes the emptiness quality of awareness, Tögal works with the 'appearance' or 'form' aspect.

Vajra (Dorje རྡོ་རྗེ་ *rdo rje*) - A Sanskrit word meaning 'thunderbolt, 'meaning indestructibe. In tantric ritual, it refers to an actual ritual object, a double-ended usually five-pronged scepter which is coupled with the tantric bell to represent the unbreakable union of Wisdom and Compassion. In the context of tantric Buddhism, the word often appears as a qualifier connoting 'non-dual.'

Vajrayana – The 'Nondual' or 'Indestructible' Vehicle, the name for esoteric, tantric Buddhism. Scholars often class Vajrayana as a separate, third vehicle of

Buddhist teachings alongside Hinayana and Mahayana, yet practitioners themselves tend to see Vajrayana as a specific, esoteric expression of Mahayana teachings and the Bodhisattva ideal, one which places strong emphasis on Guru Yoga and Empowerment. Vajrayana relies on an alchemical model where what is impure and poisonous (the afflictive emotions) can, through skillful means, be transmuted into the highest medicine and source of realization.

Vipashyana (Lhagtong ལྷག་མཐོང་ lhag mthong) - 'Direct Insight' or 'Seeing through', a form of Buddhist mental cultivation or meditation in which the meditator trains to observe all phenomena and afflictive emotions that arise without grasping. The meditator examines these phenomena impartially to realize their impermanent and dependent nature. Vipashyana, along with Shamatha represent the core components of Buddhist contemplative discipline.

View (Tawa ལྟ་བ་ lta ba) - The perspective of Ati Yoga, which recognizes and realizes the true nature of mind and all phenomena, beyond conceptuality and ordinary dualistic thinking.

Yuthok Yönten Gönpo (གཡུ་ཐོག་ཡོན་ཏན་མགོན་པོ་ g.yu thog yon tan mgon po) - 'The Turquoise Roof (Doctor), The Lord of Good Qualities'. Refers both to the original, legendary systematizer of Traditional Tibetan Medicine, Yuthok the Elder born in eighth century Tibet, and the twelfth century Tibetan yogi-doctor by the same name,

Yuthok the Younger, who continued the older master's legacy. The title 'Turquoise Roof' derives from the heaps of turquoise that were miraculously showered on the roof of Yuthok the Elder's house by water-spirits in gratitude for Yuthok having provided their father with medical treatment. Yuthok the Elder and Younger were both masters of Ati Yoga, and achieved the greater Rainbow Body.

Yuthok Nyingthig (གཡུ་ཐོག་སྙིང་ཐིག་ *g.yu thog snying thig*) - The 'Heart-essence of Yuthok', the revealed spiritual teachings of Sowa Rigpa or Tibetan Traditional Medicine. A comprehensive cycle of Vajrayana transmissions, it underwent multiple instances of editing over the centuries, as newer devotees of Yuthok experienced visions of him and received and incorporated new prayers and teachings. The Yuthok Nyingthig is a complete cycle of practices beginning with Ngöndro, progressing through Guru Yogas and Six Yogas and culminating in Ati Yoga practice. The Yuthok Nyingthig is a non-sectarian path, containing elements from all four schools of Vajrayana Buddhism and is characterized by its concise and simple methods designed to bring about the ultimate benefit of complete spiritual liberation as well as worldly benefits such as good health, improved diagnostic and treatment skills for the physician.

ABOUT THE AUTHOR

Dr. Nida Chenagtsang was born in Amdo, in North Eastern Tibet. Interested in Sowa Rigpa, the traditional healing science of his people, he began his early medical studies at the local Tibetan Medicine hospital. Later he gained scholarship entry to Lhasa Tibetan Medical University, where he completed his medical education in 1996. He completed his practical training at the Tibetan Medicine hospitals in Lhasa and Lhoka.

Alongside his medical education, Dr. Nida received complete Vajrayana Buddhist training: in the Dudjom Tersar tradition; in the Longchen Nyingthig cycle of practices from his teacher, Ani Ngawang Gyaltsen (pictured below); and in the Yuthok Nyingthig lineage, the spiritual counterpart to Sowa Rigpa, from his teachers Khenchen Troru Tsenam and Khenpo Tsultrim Gyaltsen.

Dr. Nida has published many articles and books on Sowa Rigpa (Traditional Tibetan Medicine) and the Yuthok Nyingthig tradition. He has extensively researched ancient Tibetan healing methods, and has gained high acclaim in the East and West for his revival of traditional Tibetan external healing therapies.

Dr. Nida is the Co-Founder and Medical Director of Sorig Khang International (formerly the International Academy for Traditional Tibetan Medicine) and Co-Founder of the International Ngakmang Institute, established to preserve and maintain the Rebkong ngakpa yogic culture within modern Tibetan society. He trains students in Sowa Rigpa and the Yuthok Nyingthig spiritual tradition in over 40 countries around the world.

Dr. Nida with his teacher the Yogini Ani Ngawang Gyaltsen, who transmitted to him the teachings of Ati Yoga, Mahamudra, and the Six Yogas in Lhasa, Tibet.

ABOUT SORIG KHANG INTERNATIONAL

Facing the imminent loss of Tibetan culture, philosophy, literature, science, and religion, the Sorig Khang International Foundation is to be contributing to the preservation and propagation of Traditional Tibetan Medicine. In particular, the continuity of the holistic Tibetan healing sciences in their theory and their practice, as well as in their philosophy, and in its closely connected spirituality as a complete system in the Yuthok Nyingthig transmission lineage, is to be protected.

– From the Sorig Khang International Foundation Charter

The International Academy for Traditional Tibetan Medicine was established by Dr. Nida Chenagtsang in 2006 to ensure the integrity and authenticity of *Sowa Rigpa* – Traditional Tibetan Medicine and its closely connected spiritual lineage, the Yuthok Nyingthig – and to promote the continuity of their practice. IATTM was officially established as Sorig Khang International (SKI) in 2016, an international nonprofit foundation *(stiftung)* based in Germany. Local Sorig Khang centers have been established under the direction of Dr. Nida Chenagtsang in over forty countries worldwide and offer Traditional Tibetan Medicine study and training programs, practical health education, clinical and therapeutic services, and spiritual practice and retreat opportunities to the general public.

CPSIA information can be obtained
at www.ICGtesting.com
Printed in the USA
BVOW07s0345101117
499963BV00035B/434/P